# LIZ COLLIN

# THEY'RE
# LYING

## The Media, The Left,
## and The Death of
## George Floyd

Paper Birch Press

Minneapolis, MN

# CONTENTS

If you've seen the truth be silenced,

if you've spoken out only to be ignored,

if you've ever felt hope is lost, this book is dedicated to you.

# ACKNOWLEDGMENTS

To my loyal family and friends who never let me give up...

To the people I didn't know, who believed in me when I struggled
to believe in myself...

To my colleagues at Alpha News for giving me the freedom
to speak the truth...

To my extraordinary editor who I'm blessed to call a friend...

To the brave men and women of the Minneapolis Police Department,
especially those who shared their stories...

To the people of Minneapolis, the residents and business owners who were
hurt the most by the lies...

To God who has guided me through this storm...

My most humble and sincere gratitude for making this book possible.


*Liz Collin*

# PREFACE

To understand how the lies about the arrest and death of George Floyd have affected me personally and professionally—and how my family became part of the backstory that made headlines across America—requires a bit of retrospective...

For as long as I can remember, I dreamed about being a news reporter. I grew up in small-town Minnesota and spent a lot of time with my grandparents who lived nearby. Staying up late to watch the news was a treat for me back then. Which probably explains why I started my own newspaper—when I was ten. It was called *Neighborhood News* (clever title, I know). Surprisingly, it caught on. Soon *The Daily Globe*, the real local newspaper, started mentioning articles from our little newspaper and so did the local radio station. While I'd love to think it was because of our compelling news stories, I think it had more to do with compassion and encouragement. Nonetheless, I was proud to share stories that others wanted to hear. I was captivated by journalism before I even knew what it was. I wrote articles, edited stories, and learned about life. The fact that I was in the news business while I was still in elementary school just made it even better.

About a year later, I had a truly life-changing experience, the kind that sets your course in life whether you recognize it or not. The occasional mentions of *Neighborhood News* in *The Daily Globe* caught the attention of WCCO, the news channel I watched growing up. If I wasn't already destined to be a news reporter, I was the day Don Shelby interviewed me. Shelby was the face of WCCO, and he was working on a heartfelt piece about me—the girl behind the small-town local newspaper. During the interview, Mr. Shelby asked me what I wanted to do when I grew up. I matter-of-factly replied, "I want your job."

Fourteen years later, I was doing just that. I was working alongside Don as a reporter and anchor at WCCO.

In the meantime, I grew up. I worked hard and dealt with my share of hassles just like everybody else. In high school, I helped start the student TV station. I was given keys to the school so I could use the studio whenever I wanted. I guess that said a lot about my trustworthiness, even for a small town. Along with the high school news show, I also worked at KWOA radio on weekends and during the summer. I was doing what I wanted to do, but like just about every other high-school graduate, I wanted to get out and see more of the world. So, I studied journalism in southern Florida, which was a world away from Minnesota in so many ways. After earning a degree, I started out as a reporter and anchor in Sioux Falls, and then went on to Wichita, and Harrisburg, Pennsylvania. With years of experience, I came back home to Minnesota, where I belonged, I suppose. I started working for WCCO in Minneapolis in 2008. It truly was a dream come true.

However, on May 25, 2020, my world changed—our world changed. The death of George Floyd was a perfect storm of tragic circumstances, chaos, and confusion. It was also an opportunity for power-hungry politicians, cowardly leaders, the media, and the Left to seize upon a tragedy—and hide the truth from Minneapolis and the rest of the world. Four officers were fired without due process, without any sense of fairness, and without an ounce of common sense. Riots erupted, and block after block of Minneapolis was set ablaze. Along with miles of destruction, 1,500 businesses were destroyed along with any hope for civility.[1] Tragically, four people lost their lives and were violently

---

1. Penrod, J. & Sinner, C. J. (2020, July 13). Buildings damaged in Minneapolis, St. Paul after riots. *Star Tribune.*

killed during the rioting in Minneapolis and countless others have suffered the lawlessness ever since.[2]

Everything I understood about the media and the truth seemed like it was turned upside down. The consequences really hit home when activists and police reformers tried to "cancel" my husband, Bob Kroll. As a few episodes of *COPS* from the early '90s make embarrassingly clear, Bob was always part of the action throughout his career, whether he was working as a street cop, a SWAT team member, a supervisor, or a police union leader. So, it shouldn't seem surprising that Bob was president of the police union when officers Derek Chauvin, J. Alexander Kueng, Thomas Lane, and Tou Thao were fired after their encounter with George Floyd. Bob asked for calm and cautioned against rushing to judgment. However, outraged civil-rights attorneys, social media mobs, and so-called "peaceful" protesters were obsessed with race, politics, and revenge. So according to them, since Bob shook hands with President Trump during a rally in October of 2019, of course Bob had to be a white supremacist—and had to be fired, cancelled, or killed. Due to the political outrage, Bob become a scapegoat and the face of "white supremacy in American policing" according to *Rolling Stone* magazine.[3] He was also *the reason* for racism and the riots in Minneapolis according to the ACLU (American Civil Liberties Union) of Minnesota.

It didn't take long before I also became a target of cancel culture. The fact that I was married to Bob was hardly a secret. In fact, I told the news director at WCCO about him before we even went on our first date in October 2016. I

---

2. Three of the homicide victims are referenced here: Joint Transportation and Judiciary and Public Safety Committee Minnesota Senate. (2020, October 8). *Review of lawlessness and government responses to Minnesota's 2020 Riots.* A fourth victim was seen being rescued by MPD officers during a live news broadcast but was not reported by mainstream media.
3. Volk, S. (2021, May 12). The enemy within: Race and white supremacy in American policing. *Rolling Stone.*

never wanted anyone to question my integrity, so I wanted to avoid any potential conflict of interest concerning WCCO and the police union. Bob and I had been together for years without a legitimate complaint about our relationship, even after we were married. But since activists and civil-rights attorneys just found out for themselves, our marriage became some kind of secret racist conspiracy, just like everything else that changed overnight after the arrest and death of George Floyd. While Bob was taking the blame for the riots, I became the master manipulator of news media in the Twin Cities.

According to their warped perspective of the world, since Bob "KKKroll" was a Nazi police union leader, I must be a Nazi too since I was married to him. Of course, we were doxxed and our home address and other personal information was shared all over social media. Thanks to the insanity, there were demonstrations outside the police union and the WCCO studio where I worked. Protestors, politicians, and ironically civil-rights leaders smashed piñata effigies of Bob and I in our driveway. They also scrawled disturbing messages in sidewalk chalk throughout our neighborhood. With all the hate and death threats, even simple chores like taking out the garbage and opening the mailbox became dangerous. All of this challenged my faith, my faith in humanity, and admittedly faith in myself.

Looking back, I think Bob and I made two big mistakes. First, we started blaming ourselves for everything that was happening all around us. Second, we didn't speak up loud enough when the people we trusted to tell the truth, stopped telling the truth. Our so-called leaders became way too concerned with "managing the optics" and manipulating the facts to advance their political agendas (and hide their political failures). While others stayed silent because they were afraid to be called "racist."

Having covered news stories for years, I've learned that the truth doesn't stay hidden forever. In the two years that have since passed, Bob and I have learned from our mistakes. We realized that we were just two names on a long list of people who were scapegoated and cancelled after the arrest and death of George Floyd. We also realized we had a unique perspective to expose the lies of the media and the Left. And by "the Left" I don't mean people who call themselves democrats or liberals. I'm talking about people who insist their left-wing opinions are the only opinions and persecute others because of them. I'm also talking about those who are obsessed with gaining or maintaining political power no matter the cost or consequences.

As for the book itself, I suppose more than anything it's about tracking down the truth and putting the blame where it belongs. It's about asking the tough questions—and no longer accepting deflections and dismissive answers. Along with years of interviews and research, my own firsthand experiences can also be found in the pages that follow. Hopefully, if this book achieves anything, it will make one thing clear: we need a lot more civility to understand the truth about the death of George Floyd because our so-called leaders, the media, and the Left have been lying to us all...

# INTRODUCTION

When most people talk about "the murder of George Floyd," they often start with the tragic events of May 25, 2020. That's the day Floyd was arrested and died in police custody. But it's not the day this story began—it's the day the media and the Left started lying about it. Since then, the lies have become part of one of the biggest cases of media manipulation and political corruption in American history.

As an investigative journalist, I was following the events as they unfolded, and I've been tracking down the truth ever since. Along the way, I've discovered how the viral Facebook video shows hardly anything about the circumstances that led to Floyd's encounter with the Minneapolis Police Department. It doesn't explain why Floyd and his friend Morries Hall used counterfeit bills at a convenience store in well-established Bloods gang territory.[4] It doesn't show the methamphetamine or the fentanyl that Floyd had taken, or the drug paraphernalia he had in his pocket. And it certainly doesn't explain what led to his encounter with the police or the tragic outcome.

Going through George Floyd's long criminal history isn't the point (even though much of it has been hidden from the public). But there are plenty of facts that explain the truth about his arrest, his death, and the aftermath— along with all the lies in between. For example, about a week before the video went viral and practically everybody jumped to irreversible conclusions, a woman went to a Minneapolis hospital for a sexual assault examination. She later told a police officer she had been raped by George Floyd.

---

4. Jany, L. (2021, March 15). Prosecutors cite interpersonal beef between Bloods gang members in slaying at George Floyd Square. *Star Tribune*.

This wasn't just an accusation. There was a police report. There was a rape examination.[5] There were also plenty of other details that have been kept hidden. The media and the Left have been avoiding this case. They've also been less than truthful about so many circumstances.

That's because they're lying...

They're lying about George Floyd's five-year prison sentence for aggravated robbery with a firearm in 2007 and the other crimes he committed.[6]

They're lying about how he sold over a thousand oxycodone pills during an undercover sting in 2019 and swallowed some of them when he was arrested.[7]

They're lying about George Floyd being a suspect in a rape case.

They're lying about "chokeholds" and "neck restraints," as if the Maximum Restraint Technique (MRT) that Chauvin and the three other officers used was never part of Minneapolis Police training.

And they're lying about many other facts concerning his arrest, the riots, the trials, and the political connections behind it all.

With all the lies swirling around, the truth seems almost impossible to recognize—and the media and the Left have been marching along lockstep to keep it that way.

---

5. Identity withheld (personal communication, August 29, 2022); Identity withheld (personal communication, September 2, 2022).

6. Daily Mail Staff. (2020, May 28). Exclusive: A new start turns to a tragic end for George Floyd, who moved to Minneapolis determined to turn his life around after being released from prison in Texas. *Daily Mail.*

7. Creighton, S. (2019, May 6). Narcotics violation, MP 2019-127538. Minneapolis Police Department.

This book attempts to stop them in their tracks. It reveals some of the undeniable facts and hidden truths from people who were there or caught up in the aftermath.

When former officer Derek Chauvin answered my question about the most important thing he wanted to say to the world in this book, he offered just three words: "Follow the facts."[8]

Even more telling, when former officer Thomas Lane was asked the same question, he said: "Just follow the misconceptions and the lies..."[9]

---

8. D. Chauvin (personal communication, August 16, 2022).
9. T. Lane (personal communication, July 14, 2020).

# PART I

ASSUMPTIONS & ACCUSATIONS

## The Call

Memorial Day, May 25, 2020—We just walked in the door from our weekend trip when Bob got a call from a rookie officer. As head of the police union, his phone was always ringing. But then again, as a news reporter, mine did the same and probably even more. For a lot of reasons, we tried to keep our work and home lives separate. But we still had our tell-tale signs. If something serious happened, Bob would be out the door, otherwise he'd just sort things out in his office. He listened for a minute and then shook his head as though it was nothing urgent. About 10 minutes later, he came back and explained that a couple of rookie officers arrested a guy who might have overdosed. Opioid overdoses had become tragically common in Minnesota, so it didn't seem too far out of the ordinary.

Memorial Day had come and gone, so we went back to unpacking and getting ready for the week ahead. Although, it didn't take long before Bob's phone started ringing again. Things were different this time. The guy didn't make it and was pronounced dead at the hospital. So, Bob had to go to headquarters and help the officers through the process that follows whenever there's a police shooting, in-custody death, or other critical incident. As he was leaving, I overheard him asking some of the usual questions; "Who was on scene? Any weapons? Was he resisting?"

This was all routine for him. Bob was a lieutenant and rose through the ranks in the Minneapolis Police Department (MPD). He has served on the union board longer than anyone can remember—even he can't remember sometimes. From shootings, to firing officers, to complaints and grievances, who knows how many cases he's handled in the past 20 years. He was elected union president in 2015, before we were married, so unexpected calls and interruptions have always been part of our "routine."

However, this was the last time our lives would ever seem familiar or routine again. I didn't know it at the time, but Bob was on the phone with Officer Thomas Lane. Lane and three other officers—Derek Chauvin, J. Alexander Kueng, and Tou Thao—were trying to arrest George Floyd. I also had no idea that Bob and I were about to get caught up in national headlines and become targets of cancel culture. And I had absolutely no idea that Minneapolis and the rest of America would never be the same again...

Bob left around eight or nine that night and came home around 4:30 in the morning. He said everything at headquarters seemed fine and straightforward—until Chief Arradondo showed him a video that was going viral on social media. Bob said it looked bad. Really bad. But nobody knew for sure what happened. He figured at some time later that day, they'd review the police body cam videos and maybe even a preliminary autopsy report. He was exhausted and didn't get into the details.

## The Next Morning

I was up about two hours later and started checking the news and social media like I always did. It was part of my job and part of my life, although I'm not so sure there's a line between the two. It was immediately obvious that whatever Bob had been dealing with made national headlines overnight. Even COVID hardly seemed to matter anymore. The cellphone video Bob mentioned was now everywhere on social media along with plenty of outrageous assumptions and accusations of police racism. The media instantly began pushing the outrage with never-ending speculation based on nothing more than a Facebook video. I didn't know what to think, but I knew there was a lot more to the story.

Bob woke up about an hour later. I was in "media mode" as he calls it; something like talking on the phone, texting, flipping through news channels, and taking notes all at the same time. He looked half-asleep but surprised to see the video Arradondo showed him playing on the news. I'm not sure exactly what happened next. But within minutes, it was like part of this major story was developing in my living room. There wasn't a moment when Bob didn't have his phone to his ear talking to the other union leaders, in between non-stop calls from the media. At some point, he finally told me what was happening. Bob said he met with officers Chauvin, Kueng, Lane, and Thao at headquarters and walked them through the process and the paperwork. As with any other critical incident, they were placed on administrative duty until the investigation was completed. Of course, the autopsy wasn't even started, so nobody knew which drugs were involved or the actual cause of death. But from the 911 call about a guy who was "not in control of himself,"[10] and the way the officers said he was acting, it sounded like an overdose, or case of excited delirium, or something like that.

After dealing with all the formalities, Bob left with everybody else. He was talking with the other union reps outside city hall when someone from the chief's office called and told Bob to come back upstairs immediately— Arradondo wanted him to see something. Despite all the rumors that would soon play out in the news and social media, Bob and Chief Arradondo got along fine. Arradondo, or "Rondo" as he's more commonly known, sent me a thoughtful text on Mother's Day about two weeks before. Bob would often say that out of all the police chiefs he worked with, he had the best relationship with Arradondo by far.

But when Bob went back up to Arradondo's office, the situation had changed dramatically. Arradondo wasn't saying much. Neither was John Elder, the public information officer for the department. After a few awkward minutes, Arradondo finally spoke up and said he made the decision to call in the FBI

---

10. Martinez, P. (2020, May 29). Minneapolis releases transcript of George Floyd 911 call. *CBS News*.

(The Federal Bureau of Investigation) to take over. Bob said he was speechless. This never happened before. It was completely unprecedented and totally out of character for Arradondo to make that kind of call.

For whatever reason, this became a federal case in less than ten minutes. Bob kept asking him what happened and why things had changed. Arradondo wasn't giving any straight answers—until he showed Bob a cellphone video that was going viral on social media.[11] The way the officers were trying to deal with the guy who was resisting, the way they were trying to handle the crowd, and all the insults and accusations from the bystanders—the video showed plenty of things going wrong and hardly anything that looked right. However, Bob knew that a few minutes of cellphone video hardly told the whole story. Of course, the video recordings from officers' body cameras would explain a lot more. At the very least, the videos would show what each officer did or didn't do from the moment they arrived on scene. So, Bob asked Arradondo about the body cam videos. Instead of setting up a time to review them, Arradondo just repeated that he made the decision to call in the FBI. Things weren't adding up. But it was three o'clock in the morning and downloading the body cam videos would take hours. Bob figured he'd be able to review the footage soon enough with the FBI or whoever else was involved in the investigation. He also thought it was probably a good idea to try to get some sleep in the meantime, since it was apparently going to be a long day. Besides, there wasn't much to be done without knowing all the facts. As for the information about the case, there wasn't much more than the cellphone video and a press release John Elder published earlier that night. [12]

11. Frazier, D. (Realprettymarie). (2020, May 25). Facebook. https://www.facebook.com/darnellareallprettymarie/posts/1425401580994277
12. Elder, J. (2020, May 25). Man dies after medical incident during police interaction. *The Minneapolis Police Department*.

### ###

**Man Dies After Medical Incident During Police Interaction**

May 25, 2020 (MINNEAPOLIS) On Monday evening, shortly after 8:00 pm, officers from the Minneapolis Police Department responded to the 3700 block of Chicago Avenue South on a report of a forgery in progress. Officers were advised that the suspect was sitting on top of a blue car and appeared to be under the influence.

Two officers arrived and located the suspect, a male believed to be in his 40s, in his car. He was ordered to step from his car. After he got out, he physically resisted officers. Officers were able to get the suspect into handcuffs and noted he appeared to be suffering medical distress. Officers called for an ambulance. He was transported to Hennepin County Medical Center by ambulance where he died a short time later.

At no time were weapons of any type used by anyone involved in this incident. The Minnesota Bureau of Criminal Apprehension has been called in to investigate this incident at the request of the Minneapolis Police Department.

No officers were injured in the incident.

Body worn cameras were on and activated during this incident.

The GO number associated with this case is 20-140629.

### ###

Despite what he told Bob, Arradondo didn't ask the FBI to take over the case, he asked them to "take a look" at it. As Arradondo later explained to investigators from the BCA (Bureau of Criminal Apprehension):

> "...based on what I had observed in that video [the viral cellphone video] I at least believed it was of significance that the, our FBI should... take a look."

Bob also didn't know that Arradondo had already spoken to local faith leaders, activists, and "leaders from the African American community" in those early morning hours to schedule a meeting with them later that day. As Arradondo explained in his own words, he "knew that there were many dynamics that were going to evolve" and that "by sunrise this was going to ignite a lot of emotion and what have you..."[13]

## Seizing Control of The Narrative

As Bob was telling me what happened, the situation seemed to be getting worse. The headlines were more damning and the rhetoric more hostile. At the same time, hundreds of protesters were gathering outside CUP Foods, the convenience store where Floyd used a counterfeit $20 bill. I'd been filling in as the anchor for the noon newscast on WCCO for the past several weeks and was scheduled to go into the newsroom later that morning. I checked in with my news director when I first heard about the incident. But now that the MPD was all over the news, and I was married to the leader of the police union, I thought it was a good idea to have another anchor sub for me that day—not knowing *then* I would never anchor for WCCO ever again.

Amid all the growing contempt and incivility, there was one thing that seemed rather obvious: nobody seemed to care about the facts. The video on Facebook looked bad enough. But the media and the Left were apparently trying to control the narrative and manipulate it to their advantage. There was no preliminary autopsy report, and the body cam videos still weren't released, so Bob was getting concerned. He decided to go the federation sooner rather than later to work on a press release and try to encourage civility instead of jumping to conclusions. He left sometime around ten that morning. I was

---

13. State of Minnesota v. Derek Chauvin, Exhibit 14 (August 28, 2020). Chief Arradondo was interviewed by BCA Special Agent James Reyerson and FBI Special Agent Blake Hostetter on June 11, 2020; Minnesota Department of Public Safety, Bureau of Criminal Apprehension (BCA) Case #2020-338.

alone in my element sorting through all the headlines, doing research, and trying to make some sense of it all. Sometime after Bob left that morning, MPD updated its original press release about the incident. The original didn't explain everything, as no press release could ever do, but at least it provided some details. The update, however, seemed almost cryptic:[14]

###

### Investigative Update on Critical Incident

May 26, 2020 (MINNEAPOLIS) As additional information has been made available, it has been determined that the Federal Bureau of Investigations will be a part of this investigation.

###

Clearly, this posed a lot more questions and didn't provide any answers. It didn't explain *what* information had been made available, or *why* the FBI was now part of the investigation. The update raised even more suspicion about the original press release. A growing number of people who watched the Facebook video thought the press release was an attempt to cover up the police brutality they believed they saw. The lack of information in the update didn't help. If it was meant to show transparency and accountability, it seemed to have the opposite effect. It also seemed to be a warning sign that Arradondo and MPD leaders weren't making things better, but only making things worse.

## The Unexpected

Bob and I were texting back and forth while he was at the federation. I was giving him updates about how things seemed to be falling apart by the minute. I'm not sure when exactly, but he called and told me something wasn't right. He said he spoke with Lieutenant Wheeler from IAD, the Internal Affairs

---

14. Elder, J. (2020, May 26). Investigative update on critical incident. *The Minneapolis Police Department*.

Division. Bob thought Wheeler was reaching out to tell him the body cam videos were downloaded and ready for review. Instead, Wheeler said something *completely* unexpected: all four officers were going to be fired by the end of the day. Bob said he was asking Wheeler all kinds of questions—but Wheeler didn't have any answers. Instead, it seemed like he was trying to tell Bob that his hands were tied. Bob said the whole situation seemed suspicious, as if Arradondo and Mayor Frey were up to something.

## Accountability Anyone?

Arradondo seemed to be doing a lot behind the scenes and could've been keeping Wheeler and IAD out of the loop for a reason. So, Bob called Arradondo directly hoping to get some answers. He said he started with the obvious: Why were the officers being fired? Who's leading the investigation? When are the body cam videos going to be released?

But like the night before, Bob said Arradondo just kept repeating himself without any explanation. Something wasn't right. Arradondo would typically cooperate with the union, even in the worst of situations, like the tragic shooting of Justine Damond.[15] Arradondo was Assistant Chief back then, but he kept Bob and the other union reps informed. Also, it wasn't like Arradondo to make a hasty decision, like calling the FBI in the middle of the night ten minutes after everyone left and everything seemed fine. The idea that Arradondo decided to fire the officers *without due process* was also completely out of character.

Although the most telling thing was probably this: protesters and practically everyone else were demanding accountability—but Arradondo seemed to be avoiding it. After the riots in Ferguson in 2014 and all the demands for body cams and police accountability, why would Arradondo, an African American

---

15. Forliti, A. (2022, June 25). Ex-Minneapolis officer who killed 911 caller to be released. *AP News*.

police chief, refuse to release body cam footage related to the death of a Black man who allegedly died because of police brutality? The lack of accountability and body cams were supposedly the reasons for the rioting in Ferguson and elsewhere in America at the time.[16] But now in this case, four MPD officers were each wearing a body camera. For whatever reason, Arradondo, Mayor Frey, or whoever else was pulling the strings, seemed to be delaying the release of the footage. This went against every principle of police accountability. Clearly, this was political—and it seemed like a set up.

Nevertheless, Bob was still hopeful the FBI, the BCA, or some other acronym-agency would release something before the four officers were fired. Otherwise, they were going to be terminated without due process or any official evidence whatsoever. But I don't think anyone could've predicted how long it would take before the body cam videos would be released. Worst of all, since they've been available, only a fraction of the people who watched the viral Facebook video actually watched the body cam videos—and even fewer have watched all four of them all the way through. Aside from trying to get the videos or any other evidence, Bob and the rest of the union board were scrambling to make arrangements for officers Chauvin, Kueng, Lane, and Thao, who were going to be fired in the next few hours. I was tracking the protests—but then it struck me. Bob was right; there's no way Arradondo was behind all of this. Mayor Frey was probably calling the shots, because he tried doing the very same thing before.

### Mayor Frey and "Racist" Christmas Tree Trash

As part of yearly tradition, officers decorated a Christmas tree in the lobby of the fourth precinct. However, in 2018, one particular officer was apparently a bit too proud of the decorations and would scold other officers for walking too

---

16. Culhane, S., & Schweitzer, K. (2017, January 5). Police shootings and body cameras one year post-Ferguson. *Policing & Society.*

close to it or otherwise failing to appreciate its magnificence. So, when a couple of officers (who were also accomplished pranksters) couldn't take it anymore, they went outside, picked up some trash and redecorated the tree with it. Although, maybe it's more appropriate to say they spontaneously *re-imagined* the tree according to a more urban aesthetic. You could say it was cop humor at its finest, but the joke quickly became no laughing matter. A citizen was offended and complained on social media about how the trash on the tree seemed "racist." Being offended and demanding an apology on social media was all the rage. Apparently, when Mayor Frey heard about the racist Christmas tree trash, he was furious and promised to fire the officers responsible within 24 hours.[17] Who knew that roughly 18 months later, the Christmas tree fiasco would be pivotal in trying to make sense of the political moves Frey seemed to be making behind the scenes. Obviously, there was a pattern here. In 2018, Frey apparently overreacted to accusations of "racism" and quickly promised to fire police officers within 24 hours. Now he seemed to be doing the same thing. Frey's symbolic firings say a lot about his vanity and virtue signaling on social media. They also say a lot about rushing to judgment and disregarding due process—things true leaders would never brush aside.

Having covered news stories for more than two decades, one of the things I've noticed is that overreactions and rash decisions are often signs of bigger problems. Although in this case, Mayor Frey's judgment, or the lack of it, might've been helped along by his need for attention, and his love for craft beers and microbrews. When the racist Christmas tree fiasco broke out, someone in Frey's inner-circle shared some rather telling insights with Bob: Frey apparently had more than a few beers when he heard about the racist Christmas tree scandal and decided to take action.

---

17. Flynn, M. (2018, December 3). Minneapolis police decorate Christmas tree with racial stereotypes in majority-black neighborhood. *The Washington Post.*

**Bob Knows Everybody & Everyone Else Knows Bob**

Sure, this could've been a rumor. However, Bob had been a cop for years. He started long before Frey landed in Minneapolis and won a seat on the city council. Bob knew everybody and practically everyone else knew Bob. He had more informants in more bars in the Twin Cities than most people realized, including the mayor, city council members, and who knows how many unsuspecting criminals. So according to Bob's vast network of informants, the rumor was verified by more than a few sources. But whatever Mayor Frey's state of mind or inebriation might have been, he apparently put bold promises before due process. Consequently, one of the officers who was fired was reinstated. The other was fed up with the nonsense and retired. It's difficult to understand how Frey, a former civil rights attorney, didn't seem to realize that by rushing to judgment and appeasing the demands for an apology, he was reinforcing the "racist cop narrative." Promising to fire the officers made the narrative seem true—unless of course, trash is truly racist. Apparently, Frey didn't learn his lesson. Once again, he seemed to be rushing to judgment before there was even an investigation. It also seemed like he failed to realize how firing four officers without due process—and without releasing the body cam videos—would set the city of Minneapolis on a collision course headed straight for disaster.

**It's All Who You Know...**

Speaking of politics and who you know, it's unlikely that Arradondo or any other police chief could just call the FBI at three in the morning and have them immediately take over an investigation. Mayor Frey and his fellow democrats were probably a lot better connected and far more capable. Besides, unlike Chief Arradondo, Mayor Frey and others on the Left had a lot more to gain by making this kind of political move. After all, it was an election year. The Left was dead set on ousting President Trump and other republicans. Accusing four cops of being racist made Frey and his fellow democrats look like civil rights crusaders and perfectly fit the anti-Trump agenda. Frey had plenty of connections within the Democratic party in Minnesota and beyond. Some of Frey's democrat associates included Minnesota Governor Tim Walz, Lieutenant Governor Peggy Flanagan, and Attorney General Keith Ellison, who would soon take over the prosecution of officer Derek Chauvin. As a democrat, Frey was also affiliated with US Senators Amy Klobuchar and Tina Smith, and several US Congress members including the often-controversial Ilhan Omar. About 100 Minnesota state representatives could also be counted among Frey's fellow democrats. John Thompson—who would soon be screaming about the KKK and bashing a piñata that looked like me in front of my house—was one of them.

**The Left: Demanding Accountability While Avoiding Accountability**
Thompson is just one example of how Democrats get away with never-ending demands while never doing anything wrong. For example, he was previously arrested and charged with domestic violence and making terroristic threats. He also caused a disturbance at a hospital, which had to go on lock down.[18] Not only did Thompson dodge convictions, but he was also endorsed by Governor Walz, Representative Ilhan Omar, and the Minnesota DFL. Even the news station I worked for, WCCO-TV, apparently looked the other way to help Thompson get elected. But that's just one example of how the media and the Left were taking ignorance and wrongdoing to a whole other level.

Mayor Frey, Governor Walz, and other democrats claimed the arrest and death of George Floyd was a horrific case of "systemic police racism." It happened under their leadership, but somehow, they had nothing to do with it. In hindsight, it's easier to see how politicians were creating the illusion of accountability without holding themselves accountable. Sure, Arradondo and

---

18. Hooten, K. (2020 August 23). Apparent record of dem at center of Hugo outburst shows past charges of domestic assault, terroristic threats. *Alpha News*.

Frey faced some criticism. But they also made it seem like they had *nothing* to do with pushing a divisive narrative of racism and inciting the riots that were about to erupt.

### Right & Wrong and the Rules in Between

If the outrage on the news and social media was any indication, the lack of accountability and the lack of due process didn't seem to matter. It also seemed like Chauvin and the other three officers now had to worry about a lot more than losing their jobs. Whether they would be alive tomorrow no longer seemed like something to take for granted. It didn't seem like the MPD, or the rest of Minneapolis stood much of chance either.

The most hated cops in America would soon be sitting in Bob's office. Despite the growing tensions, he was still deeply concerned that Chauvin, Kueng, Lane, and Thao were going to be fired without any official evidence or even an investigation. Although, he seemed even more concerned that the body cam videos *still* weren't released. If they were, at least more of the story would be plain to see. I understood his concerns. Just being around him, I learned more about the details of firing an officer than I ever wanted to know. Given his role as a leader of the police union, due process was a primary concern. I didn't have much of a choice in hearing about all of this. But now that Mayor Frey promised to fire all four officers and was calling for criminal charges, I had a new-found appreciation for evidence, due process, and all the other things Bob was always talking about.

When officers were fired or disciplined, Bob and the other union leaders had to make sure it was done according to protocol. When somebody does something wrong, it had to be handled the right way, even in the worst cases of police misconduct, greed, or stupidity. As the president of the police union, Bob had to make sure *the process* was right. He was like a referee making sure there'd be a fair fight and that both sides were playing by the rules. From Bob's perspective, there's right and wrong—and the rules in between. He's handled the firing of dozens of police officers over the years and hundreds of demotions and cases of discipline. He's even dealt with some of his own. So, firing four officers wasn't an issue for Bob. It was *how* they were being fired that was his main concern.

Mayor Frey's demands went against every protocol. Even when an officer is accused of the most obvious bogus complaint, there's always a preliminary investigation at the very least. In this case, there was none of that. Four police officers were basically being fired because Mayor Frey said so. As a former civil rights attorney, Frey must have known that he was ignoring one of the most fundamental principles of justice in America: the principle of being innocent until proven guilty.

**Mayor Frey: "I Believe What I Saw"**

Frey was holding press conferences throughout the day and quoting himself on social media in between. The whole time he was making the situation all about race. When he told the media and the public that the four officers were going to be fired, his announcement was filled with drama more than anything else:[19]

> "For five minutes, we watched as a white officer pressed his knee to the neck of a black man."

Instead of promoting calm and civility, Frey basically condemned the officers as executioners when he said:

> "Being Black in America should not be a death sentence."

---

19. Sanchez, R., Sutton, J., & Moshtaghian, A. (2020, May 26). Minneapolis cops fired after video shows one kneeling on neck of black man who later died. *CNN.*

At one point, Frey seemed so tangled up in his own self-righteousness that he basically dismissed the investigation:

> "Whatever the investigation reveals, it does not change the simple truth, he [George Floyd] should still be with us this morning... I believe what I saw and what I saw is wrong on every level."

Sure, there's something to be said for "seeing is believing." Although the wiser among us know "things aren't always what they appear to be" and that there's often "more than meets the eye." Nonetheless, Frey was making some damning accusations based on prejudgment and prejudice. Even *The New York Times*, the liberal party press, took notice:[20]

> "After Mr. Floyd's death, Mr. Frey took the unusual step of bluntly criticizing the actions of the police officers on social media before an investigation had been completed."

Frey's prejudiced self-promotion embroiled Minneapolis and the rest of America in a mythical racial conflict—and none of it was necessary. His accusations were like an open invitation for all the violence that would soon break out. As if the investigation or the autopsy wouldn't reveal the actual cause of death or any other details, Frey seemed to be telling the world, it's okay to bash police officers based on what you *believe*—facts be damned.

### Outrage & The ACLU

By now it was clear that any sense of reason and civility had been abandoned. Hardly any of the facts were known, but people were jumping to conclusions and formulating conspiracies. Just about every race-based accusation automatically became a fact. For example, the ACLU (American Civil Liberties Union) issued a press release titled "ACLU Responds to Minneapolis Police

---

20. Stockman, F. (2020, May 29). Mayor Jacob Frey of Minneapolis had promised to improve police relations. *The New York Times*.

Killing George Floyd."[21] They called for "a fair, independent, and transparent investigation," but how could that be possible with "killing" in the headline?

Apparently, the ACLU had already tried the case in the court of public opinion. It was a "killing"—as if nothing else could possibly explain what happened. The ACLU seemed to be inviting outrage:

> "We need you with us to build national pressure and ensure public outrage leads to action."

Obviously, this was political. But the next sentence shows how the ACLU was also being irresponsible:

> "In a 10-minute-long eyewitness video that eerily recalls the Eric Garner case in New York City, a Minneapolis police officer can be seen kneeling directly on Floyd's neck, crushing it into the pavement."

"Crushing it into the pavement"—that's a factual description? You'd expect this kind of hyperbole from kids in elementary school, not an organization that claims to protect civil rights. The ACLU proclaims that it "dares to create a more perfect union beyond one person, party, or side." However, in their press release, the ACLU seemed to be doing exactly that. Along with ironically trouncing upon the civil liberties of the four officers, the ACLU was calling for "national pressure" so that one *very specific* and supposedly "independent" attorney general could prosecute this case—Keith Ellison, the democrat attorney general of Minnesota:

> "Please join us in calling on Minnesota leadership to hand the case over to an independent prosecutor under the Attorney General's authority."

---

21. American Civil Liberties Union, ACLU of Minnesota. (2020, May 26). ACLU responds to Minneapolis Police killing George Floyd.

If the ACLU supports democracy, then it's hard to understand why they
seemed to be ignoring the principle of being innocent until proven guilty. Or
why—with prejudice and without even knowing any of the facts—they were
apparently drumming up "national pressure" and "public outrage." Or why
they already seemed to be laying the groundwork to influence an investigation
and potential trial by using the full force of the state of Minnesota. Unless of
course, this was all for their political benefit. What's even worse, the ACLU,
Governor Walz, and others on the Left seemed to be conspiring to give
authority in this case to Attorney General Keith Ellison, who openly supports
Antifa.

"Antifa" supposedly stands for "anti-fascists." Although it might as well stand
for the antithesis of democracy and common sense considering all the things
this confused coalition of left-wing fanatics do and say. In 2018, when Ellison
was the deputy chairman of the Democratic National Committee, he proudly
shared a photo of himself holding a copy of "ANTIFA: The Anti-Fascist
Handbook" on Twitter.[22] Like most cowardly politicians who run and hide
whenever someone challenges the reality of their political ideas, Ellison
deleted his tweet after intense backlash. But even two years later, many were
worried about having a self-proclaimed Antifa supporter leading the
investigation. Some were also *very concerned* about how Ellison's role as the
prosecutor in the case would upend law and order in Minnesota, as this re-
tweet from Crime Watch Minneapolis shows.

---

22. See: Associated Press. (2018, January 5). Rep. Keith Ellison draws fire for tweet about Antifa
handbook and Trump. *Chicago Tribune.*

**CrimeWatchMpls**
@CrimeWatchMpls

This needs to be shared far and wide. This is our very own #MN Attorney General, @keithellison @AGEllison proudly promoting a group that is now destroying our state. This #MNDFL POS needs to be driven from office and driven from the state of #Minnesota.

♡ 495   11:26 AM - May 30, 2020

*Commentary and a re-tweet of Ellison's since-deleted support for Antifa (courtesy of Crime Watch Minneapolis (@CrimeWatchMpls).*

Maybe this was Minnesota politics (or corruption) as usual. But should we just ignore how the ACLU was calling for "national pressure" for an Antifa-loving attorney general? The ACLU claims to fight for those "whose rights have been violated." But this press release hardly reflects the right to a fair trial "by an impartial jury" according to the Sixth Amendment. Publicly condemning police officers or anyone else before an investigation has even started blatantly defies the Fifth Amendment right to not be "deprived of life, liberty, or property, without due process of law."

## The Racist, Mixed-race Group of Officers

The ACLU was apparently involved in mythmaking. In publishing this press release on their website, the ACLU included a list of related issues such as "Racial Justice" and "Racial Profiling" (just below their contact info and "donate" button, of course). How any of these issues apply to a mixed-race group of officers is something the ACLU has yet to explain. Since the media and the Left were ignoring the obvious, maybe it's worth pointing it out:

Officer Chauvin is White.

Officer Kueng is Black.

Officer Lane is White.

And Officer Thao is Hmong American (Asian).[23]

Obviously, they were a mixed-race group of Minneapolis police officers. So accusing Chauvin, Kueng, Lane, and Thao of being part of "systemic police racism" should seem ridiculous. Kueng and Lane were assigned to the 911 call—and were the first mixed-race group of officers at the scene. Chauvin and Thao were nearby and decided to help—and were the second mixed-race

---

23. Karnowski, S. (2022, January 25). Explainer: Who are 3 officers on trial in Floyd's killing? *AP News*.

group of officers to arrive. So, the idea that two mixed-race groups of officers were "racial profiling" seems to be part of an even bigger lie, if not a fabricated myth that civil rights attorneys and organizations like the ACLU depend upon for money and merit.

### Me and My Self-importance

Unfortunately, Frey and the ACLU weren't alone in pushing seemingly racist assumptions and divisive rhetoric. Politicians, celebrities, and attention-seekers of every stripe were tripping over each other to weigh in on the situation. Members of the Minnesota democratic party were also busy attempting to seize political advantage during a presidential election year. Based on nothing more than a viral video on social media, they had no idea about the facts in this case. Their non-stop virtue-signaling seemed more like propaganda for condemning anything that had to do with law and order, as if that was ever a bad thing.

For example, Minnesota senator Amy Klobuchar seemed to be calling attention to herself when she tweeted about what she called "*my* statement on the officer-involved death in Minneapolis."[24] She was seemingly adding fuel to the fire and increasing racial tensions:

> "We heard his repeated calls for help. We heard him say over and over again that he could not breathe. And now we have seen yet another horrifying and gutwrenching [sic] instance of an African American man dying."

Klobuchar also expressed her support for Mayor Frey and the "calls for immediate action." Much like the backward rhetoric from her fellow democrats, she concluded *her* statement by stating:

---

24. Klobuchar, A. (2020, May 26). *My statement on the officer-involved death in Minneapolis* [Tweet] Twitter. https://t.co/HUoGfXEj7R; emphasis added.

> "There must be a complete and thorough outside investigation into what occurred, and those involved in this incident must be held accountable."

Klobuchar was apparently following the protocol for left-wing justice: condemn and demand accountability (as if the results of the investigation were already a given). According to Senator Klobuchar's rhetoric, reasonable doubt, due process, or the idea of being innocent until proven guilty didn't stand a chance. Her anxious tweets also show how the legislative branch didn't want to be left out of the media spotlight. Ten members of the Minnesota House of Representatives wrote a letter to Governor Walz. In what sounded like an echo of the demands from the ACLU, and Klobuchar, the state reps explained how their constituents, "especially constituents of color have lost faith in the ability of Hennepin County Attorney Mike Freeman to fairly and impartially investigate and prosecute" the cases against the four officers.[25]

This wasn't satire. This was real. State legislators, the people elected to make the laws in Minnesota, were trying to influence the outcome of a jury trial. But it was also a threat to every freedom-loving person in the state. Legislators were trying to influence the executive branch to take over the case and switch prosecutors in the judicial branch. That alone is a catastrophe for democracy. And it should have been a warning sign that evidence no longer stood a chance against mob mentality. Every level and branch of Minnesota state government was now trying to influence the outcome of this case all because of what people *believed* they saw in a Facebook video.

### Ben Crump & More Hostile Rhetoric

As if there wasn't enough chaos that day, civil rights attorney Ben Crump joined the media frenzy. Crump issued a press release on Twitter to announce

---

25. Lee, F., R. Dehn, S. Jordan, et al., (2020, May 29). Release: Minneapolis delegation sends letter to Governor Tim Walz. *Minnesota House of Representatives.*

that he was now representing the family of George Floyd. Crump gained fame and considerable fortune representing the family of Trayvon Martin in 2012. Martin was killed by a Hispanic civilian, not a cop. But that didn't stop Crump from gaining celebrity status,[26] and #BlackLivesMatter from becoming a social justice movement for Marxist police reforms. Although, perhaps the most significant thing that Crump and BLM have in common is how they exploit racism as a form of *fear* and *guilt* for their own benefit. Incidentally, Crump fought alongside BLM for "justice" for Michael Brown, Terrence Crutcher, and Breonna Taylor. As in his previous cases, Crump's move to seize the narrative about "systemic police racism" turned out to be quite profitable. In this case, George Floyd's family would eventually be awarded an eye-popping $27 million-dollar settlement.

## Scoring Points in the Court of Public Opinion

In his initial press release, or "Media Alert" as he called it, Crump declared:[27]

> "Nationally renowned civil rights and personal injury attorney Ben Crump has been retained by the family of George Floyd, a man who died in the custody of the Minneapolis Police Department on May 25 when he was pinned to the ground by his neck... Floyd was stopped for a non-violent forgery charge when police detained and *killed* him."

Ironically, yet another civil rights attorney seemed to be offering up more prejudice. Unless Crump performed the autopsy himself, there's no way he could have known what "killed" George Floyd. Also, stressing the fact that Floyd was "stopped for a non-violent forgery charge" is an obvious attempt to downplay the crime Floyd committed and the reason for his arrest. However,

---

26. Martinez, A. (2020, July 20). How Florida's Ben Crump became the go-to attorney for Trayvon Martin, George Floyd cases," *Tampa Bay Times*, July 20, 2020.

27. Crump, B. (2020, May 26). *Media alert: National civil rights attorney Ben Crump retained to represent family of George Floyd, man killed by Minneapolis Police* [Tweet]. Twitter. Deleted.

it doesn't explain the counterfeit $20 bills that were stuffed between the seats inside the car where Floyd and his drug dealer Morries Hall were sitting. It doesn't explain why they were using them in a convenience store in well-known gang territory. Downplaying criminal behavior is something civil rights attorneys do a lot these days. But Crump was apparently making up the facts with his next claim:

> "We all watched the horrific death of George Floyd on video as witnesses begged the police officer to take him into the police car and get off his neck. This abusive, excessive and inhumane use of force cost the life of a man who was being detained by the police for questioning about a non-violent charge. We will seek justice for the family of George Floyd, as we demand answers from the Minnesota [sic] Police Department. How many "while black" deaths will it take until the racial profiling and undervaluing of black lives by police finally ends?"

None of this really has anything to do with the facts. For example, Floyd never asked any officer to get off his neck—which seems rather telling. Again, Floyd wasn't "detained," he was under arrest. And Crump's reference to *the* police officer" is just as absurd as his claim about "racial profiling"—actually, there were four MPD officers involved: a Black officer, two White officers, and a Hmong American officer. If those four officers were actually "racial profiling," then Crump and everybody else who jumped to the same conclusion have plenty of explaining to do. Also, Crump's mention of "black lives," as in Black Lives Matter, probably wasn't a coincidence, especially since Crump and BLM were apparently using similar social media tactics. Crump's "Media Alert" seemed to be an opening salvo and a cue for BLM and their supporters to put his call for "justice" on full blast.

## The Firing of Four Officers

Officers Chauvin, Kueng, Lane, and Thao were officially terminated sometime around six o'clock on Tuesday, less than 24 hours after they first encountered George Floyd.[28] There was plenty of paperwork, but as Bob explained, there were only two important things that needed to be done. First, each of the officers had to sign a termination letter. Second, they had to decide whether to fight to get their jobs back and file a grievance. All four of them signed their termination letters, but only three filed grievances.

Lane, who initially called Bob after they thought George Floyd overdosed, was particularly upset. He jumped in the ambulance to help resuscitate Floyd, so he could hardly make sense of the allegations that he did nothing to help. Kueng and Thao couldn't understand the situation either. They were accused of being a part of "systemic police racism," yet they were both minorities, so none of this made any sense to them. It also didn't make any sense to Bob. In the 24 years of serving the police union, he never saw anything like this. All the boxes were checked on their termination letters, but that was it. There were no investigative findings. There wasn't even an explanation—not even a sentence about why they were being fired. For example, Lane was fired because of "MPD P/P Sections 5-102.01, 5-105, 5-303.01.5-303, 5-300, 5-301, 5-304, 5-305." There wasn't any connection between the laundry list of numbers and any real evidence. So, Lane, Kueng, and Thao asked the union to file grievances on their behalf.

## Chauvin and the Police Union Parted Ways

Like the other officers, Chauvin also couldn't make any sense of the disconnect between the facts and the outrageous accusations. He had no intention to kill anybody and neither did the three other officers. He knew they weren't using

---

28. Chauvin was fired and officially discharged from the Minneapolis Police Department on May 26, 2020 at 6:15 pm; Thao at 6:30 pm; Kueng at 6:45 pm; and Lane at 7 pm.

chokeholds—like Chief Arradondo and other witnesses would later insist during his trial—they were using the Maximum Restraint Technique (MRT). This was covered in policy 5-316, which oddly wasn't listed on their termination forms. MPD officers were trained to use the MRT to deal with people who were physically resisting and experiencing a drug overdose or excited delirium and possible cardiac arrest. However, with more than 18 years on the job, Chauvin knew that facts were one thing, and optics were another. He didn't want to file a grievance and didn't want to fight to get his job back. Bob said it wasn't like an admission of guilt, it was more like a calm acceptance of outrageous circumstances. He told Bob that Arradondo had discussed the incident with local leaders and church pastors, which certainly seemed like an improper termination and nothing that even remotely followed basic protocol for an investigation. But Chauvin also said that with all the hate and outrage blowing up, he knew he could never put on a Minneapolis Police uniform again.

In many ways, Chauvin's situation seemed a lot like what Officer Darren Wilson went through in Ferguson in 2014. Officer Wilson was attacked by robbery suspect Michael Brown. Wilson was immediately found "guilty" by the media, and the lies and accusations sparked riots and unrest. Consequently, Wilson was investigated by several different agencies. None found that he did anything wrong. He was also exonerated twice and never indicted. Nonetheless, Wilson knew he could never work as a police officer ever again, or even work at all. Due to the racist accusations and the riots that followed, Wilson said he was simply "unemployable."[29] Chauvin apparently had the same realization. He also had the foresight to know that even if he could return to work, he'd be targeted and tormented on every call. He seemed to know that his presence could create never-ending conflicts for himself and

---

29. Halpern, J. (2015, August 3). The cop. *The New Yorker*; Kaufman, D. (2015, September 16). You want to fix Ferguson start with facing the facts! *New York Post*.

other officers. When Bob asked Chauvin about filing a grievance, Chauvin flatly said, "Don't do it." Since he didn't want to file a grievance, Chauvin and the police union no longer had any official relationship. Chauvin wasn't fighting to get his job back, neither was the union—and neither was Bob. But you'd never know it from watching the news or reading anything on social media. The media and the Left not only ignored the facts; they viciously kept insisting the opposite was true.

## Mayor Frey: The Right Call?

About an hour after they were fired, Frey symbolically tweeted:[30]

> "Four responding MPD officers involved in the death of George Floyd have been terminated. This is the right call."

Frey's tweet garnered thousands of "likes" and "retweets." Although this probably had less to do with his popularity, and more to do with the fact that he was stirring contempt for the Minneapolis Police Department—a department under his direct control, by the way. If that's not a political move, I'm not sure what is. Frey's never-ending comments throughout the day might have helped him side-step accountability. But his obsessive focus on racial discrimination—to the exclusion of any other possible cause of death—didn't help. Instead of urging calm and reason, Frey was stoking outrage that would soon set Minneapolis ablaze.

## From Rhetoric to Riots

Frey's grandstanding was only part of the problem. The accusations of racial discrimination and the growing tensions were about to destroy the department and the city at any moment. Arradondo, Frey, Walz, and other so-called leaders were promoting a divisive narrative and not much else. In some way or

---

30. Frey, J (@MayorFrey). (2020, May 26). *Four responding MPD officers involved in the death of George Floyd have been terminated* [Tweet]. *Twitter*.
https://twitter.com/MayorFrey/status/1265359374010273792

another, every single MPD officer was now part of a scheme of "systemic police racism." The union leaders knew they had to say something, so Bob published a statement on behalf of the union and its members:

**Statement by the Police Officers Federation of Minneapolis**

Now is not the time rush to judgement and immediately condemn our officers.

An in-depth investigation is underway. Our officers are fully cooperating.

We must review all video. We must wait for the medical examiner's report.

Officers' actions and training protocol will be carefully examined after the officers have provided their statements.

The Police Officers Federation of Minneapolis will provide full support to the involved officers.

We ask that the community remain calm and let the investigation be completed in full.

If anything made Bob a target and a scapegoat, it was this. The backlash was severe. Bob was speaking up for every MPD officer and the four officers who were fired before an investigation had even started. They were a group of mixed-race officers. But the media and the Left ignored that obvious fact and labelled Bob a "white supremacist," a "Nazi," and a whole lot worse. Of course, since I was married to him, I would soon be called "Nazi Barbie," and "Eva Braun" (the wife of Adolf Hitler who committed suicide), and other horrible things I will never repeat. Meanwhile, the so-called "peaceful protesting" throughout Minneapolis was about to turn into a full-scale riot.

# PART II

## OUTRAGE & RIOTS

**Outrage in The Streets & Tweets**

It's hard to pinpoint exactly when the riots erupted in Minneapolis. Many news sources say the rioting and looting started around six o'clock on Tuesday, the day after George Floyd was arrested and died. This was around the same time when Chauvin, Kueng, Lane, and Thao were fired—and police officers were trapped in a squad car surrounded by rioters near 38th and Chicago Ave.[31] It's also hard to say whether outrage on social media was stoking outrage in the streets, or vice versa. That morning, there were a few dozen protesters outside CUP Foods, where Floyd was arrested and died in police custody.[32] The crowd steadily grew larger and louder throughout the day. By nightfall, there were thousands of protesters in the streets throughout Minneapolis, including hundreds outside the Third Precinct, where officers Chauvin, Kueng, Lane and Thao had been assigned.[33]

The protestors were supposedly "peaceful," and many of them were. But those who were looting stores, hurling rocks, starting fires, and damaging police cars certainly were not. In turning a blind eye, Governor Walz ultimately blamed "outsiders" for all the damage and destruction. He also blamed white supremacists and drug cartels.[34] Walz may have been confused, since only 16% of those arrested during the riots had addresses outside of Minnesota.[35] However, Walz was right—the riots were being influenced by "outsiders." Although they probably weren't the ones he had in mind. While violence was

---

31. Review of lawlessness and government responses to Minnesota's 2020 Riots. (2020, October 8). *Joint Transportation and Judiciary and Public Safety Committee Minnesota Senate.*

32. Body camera video recordings of Thomas Lane and J. Alexander Kueng, Minneapolis Police Department (May 25, 2020); Thomas Lane bodycam video of George Floyd death. (2020, August 10). *Fox 9 KMSP.*

33. Thorbecke, C. (2020, May 27). Protesters clash with Minneapolis police following death of black man seen pinned down in video. *ABC News.*

34. Harris, S. (2020, May 30). Officials blame outsiders for violence in Minnesota but contradict one another on who is responsible. *The Washington Post.*

35. Belcamino, K. (2020, May 30). Majority of those arrested in George Floyd protests and riots gave Minnesota addresses. *Pioneer Press.*

breaking out across the city, left-wing politicians across the country seemed to be promoting outrage. For example, U. S. Representative Alexandria Ocasio-Cortez was certainly an outsider who seemed to be interfering and promoting more tension and unrest. She might be America's greatest attention-seeking performance-artist/politician.[36] She's also great at unintentionally revealing the tactics of the far Left.[37] She supposedly represents a district in New York about 1,200 miles away from Minneapolis. Obviously, she was an "outsider" according to Walz' definition. In the middle of all the tension and chaos, she tweeted:[38]

> "Police shootings are now a leading cause of death for young men *across the board* in the US. For Black men and boys, the risk of being killed by police is *1 in 1,000.* 1 in 1,000. Terrifying and indefensible."

Never mind that fentanyl overdoses killed more adults between 18 and 45 in 2020 than cancer, motor vehicle accidents, COVID-19, suicide, and gun violence,[39] Ocasio-Cortez was trying to call attention to herself by (mis)quoting research. But she wasn't making any sense. George Floyd wasn't shot by the police, so the connection seems a bit strange. But if she read the study, she would have noticed that the lead author noted a significant caveat that contradicts her bold claim. The author wrote:[40]

---

36. Marcus, D. (2022, July 26). The left is starting to realize AOC is just a performance artist. *New York Post.*

37. Wallace, D. (2022, July 25). NY liberal lawmaker rips AOC as 'absent' from home district after 'performative' Supreme Court stunt." *Fox News.*

38. Palmer, E. (2020, May 27). Alexandria Ocasio-Cortez weighs in on George Floyd's Death, criticizes 'Impunity of police violence.' *Newsweek.*

39. Conklin, A. (2021, December 16). Fentanyl overdoses become No. 1 cause of death among US adults, ages 18-45: 'A national emergency.' *Fox News*; see also Murphy, S. L., et. al. (2021). "Mortality in the United States, 2020," National Center for Health Statistics Data Brief No. 427.

40. Williams, J. P. (2019, August 5). Study: Police violence a leading cause of death for young men. *US News.*

"I want to be clear: When we talk about the leading causes, police violence trails behind some causes that are killing many, many people... Relative to all causes of death, it's not that frequent."

So according to the author of the study, police violence is "not that frequent." Nevertheless, Ocasio-Cortez and other left-wing politicians were dramatically portraying the opposite. Aside from their misleading messages, their timing couldn't have been worse. The last thing Minneapolis and the rest of America needed that night were more unfounded racist accusations against the police.

**Misplaced Responsibility**

But let's take her word for it: police shootings are a leading cause of death for young men, and "Black men and boys" are at an even greater risk. Not to dive into statistics, but even just a brief comparison shows how the media and the Left manipulate reality and use numbers to lie about anything that doesn't fit their narrative. *The Washington Post* police shooting database is a popular source for left-wing journalists and pundits. It indicates that in 2019, out of all the Black men between the ages of 18 and 29 in America, 103 were fatally shot by police. Out of these 103, 99 of them were armed. In other words, 96% of the Black men shot and killed by law enforcement in 2019 were armed, according to *The Washington Post*. As though picking up a gun or a knife couldn't *possibly* increase the risk of a fatal encounter with law enforcement, somehow the police are to blame for everything.

For comparison, FBI crime data indicates that 2,906 "Black or African American" males were tragically killed by other civilians in 2019. Just to be clear, 103 Black men were shot and killed by law enforcement—and 2,906 were killed by homicide offenders. But somehow police shootings are a leading cause of death? For an even broader comparison, FBI data also shows that 2,906 "Black or African Americans," both men and women, were murdered in 2019. Out of these 2,906 Black murder victims, 2,574 were killed by Black offenders. In other words, 89%—or 9 out of 10 Blacks—were killed by other Blacks. The unfortunate reality is that Blacks pose a far greater risk to themselves than fatal encounters with the police, according to FBI data.

### Black Murder Victims and Offenders (2019)

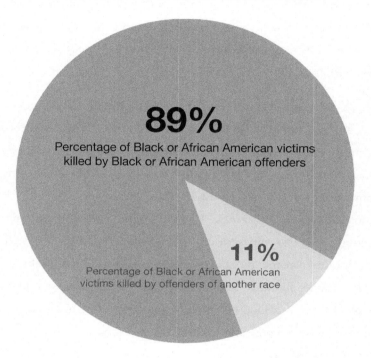

*Source: FBI Uniform Crime Reporting (UCR), Expanded Homicide Data Table 6, 2019 Crime in the United States, US Department of Justice, Federal Bureau of Investigation, Criminal Justice Information Services Division.*

Politicians tend to ignore this tragic reality. Although, criminal justice professionals and social commentators have been trying to call attention to it for years. For example, author Heather Mac Donald warned about the facts concerning race and crime in several of her writings, including her books *The War on Cops*, and *The Diversity Delusion*.[41] Yet the media and the Left don't seem to care. Apparently, their divisive narratives about race are far more important—and few politicians have been willing to *actually* do something about the realities of crime in America.

Although, Ocasio-Cortez is still right about one thing. It is absolutely "terrifying and indefensible" that people would put themselves and others in their community at risk. Common sense will tell you that the risk of a fatal encounter with the police can be drastically reduced just by complying with police commands and not committing a crime. Following the "logic" and the connections she was trying to make leads to a significant and undeniable fact: George Floyd could've easily reduced his risk of a fatal encounter with police by not committing a crime, by not resisting arrest—and by not taking methamphetamines, fentanyl, and other drugs—as the autopsy report would soon reveal. Of course, nobody wanted to talk about that, or even suggest that people are somehow responsible for their own actions.

At the same time, the media and the Left weren't just ignoring facts and making outrageous excuses, they were labeling each and every cop in Minneapolis a racist—much like the "ACAB" (All Cops Are Bastards) graffiti that showed up on buildings, sidewalks, and practically everywhere else throughout the city. Beyond the stereotypes, however, listening to what they went through tells a different side of the story.

---

41. Mac Donald, H. (2010). *The war on cops*. Encounter Books; see also Mac Donald, H. (2018). *The diversity delusion: How race and gender pandering corrupt the university and undermine our culture*. St. Martin's Press.

**Interpretation Versus Intent**

Lieutenant Kim Voss, a former commander with the Minneapolis Police Department experienced her share of scapegoating during the riots. She was also accused of being a racist about a month before the riots started. In hindsight, her experience seems like an obvious warning sign. It all started when Kim was cleaning out some storage space. Inside one of the many boxes of clutter, she found an old t-shirt, probably from the late '90s or so, with the phrase "Our day starts when your day ends" printed on it. Back then, if you walked into any homicide unit in any major city, you wouldn't have to look very far to find the phrase on a coffee mug or a stress ball. More recently, the phrase popped up in a few episodes of *Bosch*. Along with the long-lost gallows humor, the t-shirt also had a rather obvious typo: "Minneapolis Police Homocide Division." The nostalgia and the stupidity were too much for Kim, so she shared a picture of the t-shirt with her friends on Facebook with the following description:[42]

> "Attempting to organize the storage room and came across this gem! It pays to proofread before you hit 'print'."

As with just about everything on social media, the original intent was replaced with far-fetched misinterpretation. Leslie Redmond, the president of the Minneapolis NAACP complained about Kim's Facebook post. Redmond said she was "disturbed" by the idea that a high-ranking MPD commander would "make a potentially homophobic and racially charged remark." Redmond further explained:

> "I do not think this was about the misspelling of the word homicide [...] This is extremely insensitive, especially considering the involved demographics."

---

[42] Jany, L. (2020, March 31). Minneapolis police commander apologizes for sharing photo of T-shirt deemed insensitive. *Star Tribune.*

Like something out of the movie *Sixth Sense*, apparently Redmond can see people and demographics others cannot. Kim never mentioned anyone or any "demographics" and neither did the t-shirt. Nevertheless, Chief Arradondo was made aware of Redmond's clairvoyant accusations and her opinion. Since Redmond claimed to be offended, Arradondo reassured the world that the decades-old t-shirt did not reflect "the values and transformational culture that we are as a department today." Since apologies are absolutely necessary whenever someone claims to be offended, Chief Arradondo said he was sorry:

> "That item does not exist in any part of our current MPD... As Chief, I want to apologize to those we serve for any hurt or distrust this image has caused."

These days, apologies tend to bring about more trouble than understanding. So, it was hardly surprising that Redmond, the Minneapolis NAACP president, and civil-rights attorney Nekima Levy Armstrong apparently disregarded the apology and demanded a meeting with Arradondo. Exactly how a t-shirt with a typo amounts to a civil-rights issue remains unclear. Never mind that homicide divisions are necessary because people kill one another, Kim's Facebook post was a much more urgent matter. Unfortunately, this kind of rhetoric should be expected from the likes of Levy Armstrong, an advisor to Black Lives Matter, and a professional whose livelihood seemingly depends upon civil rights violations, whether real or imagined.

### The Disconnect Between Victims and Offenders

Aside from making wild accusations and labeling Kim a racist homophobe, there was even more hypocrisy in all of this. For quite some time, mentioning the race of a homicide *victim* — and the race of the *offender* — when both were "people of color" was something everyone seem to avoid. Likewise, Redmond and Levy Armstrong were calling attention to their "outrage," but they were apparently ignoring the unfortunate facts about homicide and race in

Minneapolis. Tragically, between 2010 and 2020, most homicide victims have been "Blacks" — and were killed by other "Blacks."[43] Redmond let this fact slip when she proclaimed the t-shirt was offensive "considering the involved *demographics*" even though the t-shirt didn't mention or identify anyone or any group by name. Kim already apologized for any misunderstanding she may have caused with the photo and her Facebook post. But Redmond and Levy Armstrong were seemingly relentless. They continued to criticize Kim, Levy Armstrong even going so far as to dismiss Kim's intentions:[44]

> "Her intentions do not matter. What matters most is the outcome of the actions... As a leader within the Minneapolis Police Department she should have known that posting such an offensive message on social media would be highly offensive ... not to mention to [sic] undermine public trust."

## When A Civil Rights Attorney Ignores Intent...

Whenever a civil rights attorney and law professor proclaims "intentions do not matter" every single person in America should take note. The word *intent* appears in more than 800 Minnesota legal statutes, so obviously, intent matters. Ironically, *intent* determines the definitions and degrees of murder and manslaughter.[45] So proclaiming that "intentions do not matter" seems to defy fundamental aspects of law and justice in America. But that didn't stop Levy Armstrong from condemning Kim and demanding retribution. After Arradondo met with Redmond and Levy Armstrong, Kim was demoted. Much like the Christmas tree fiasco, Mayor Frey and Chief Arradondo were apparently quick to appease any racist accusations without much regard for

43. Rosario, R. (2010, August 14). Young black men bear brunt of murder rate in Minneapolis. *Pioneer Press*; Canaparo, G., & Kassal, A. (2022, April 12). Who suffers the most from crime wave? *The Heritage Foundation.*

44. McNeff, J. (2020, April 14). Minneapolis commander demoted after Facebook post involving police humor offends NAACP. *Law Officer.*

45. Minnesota Statutes, 2021, §609.18; 609.185; 609.19; 609.195; 609.20; 609.205.

facts or investigating the actual circumstances. An opinion was apparently enough to get them to take immediate action. All of this provides a glimpse of the political environment inside the Minneapolis Police Department before the riots. So, it's hardly surprising that Frey and Arradondo would over-react and completely abandon their responsibilities when the riots broke out and real problems showed up. As Kim explained:

"Anybody with a set of balls and a backbone could have explained how a photo of a t-shirt wasn't racist at all. It wouldn't have changed everybody's mind. But maybe it would've been enough to make some people think twice before jumping to conclusions. Instead, MPD leadership gave in to the accusations and it became national news."

One of the bigger issues, according to Kim and other officers, was that MPD's top brass kept giving in to cancel culture by default. Nobody was there to support the officers, which was another problem. It wasn't like the city council was going to step in and stand up for them. Meanwhile, plenty of officers expressed their support for Kim behind closed doors, but they were afraid to do so out in the open due to fear of retribution and getting demoted themselves. Kim was also cancelled and didn't get any support from the powers that be in dealing with any of that. Social media trolls posted her home address, phone numbers, email addresses, and pictures of her kids all over the internet. They ruined her credit by signing her up for all kinds of credit cards. They subscribed her to hundreds of bizarre magazines and online dating sites using her personal info. She laughs about being signed up as "Cowgirl 911" on FarmersOnly.com. However, the death threats, were no laughing matter.

**Interview with Kim Voss (Police Supervisor)**

Kim experienced her share of awful situations during the riots. Like so many other police officers who shared their stories, she felt the lack of leadership and the hypocrisy were the worst.[46] When you're talking about riots that left block after block of Minneapolis in ruins, that's saying a lot. Kim explained some of her experiences during the rioting in her own words...

"I have a lot of memories I'm trying to repress, but I clearly remember when all of this started that Monday, Memorial Day (May 25, 2020). Around eight-thirty or so that night, we get this alert from dispatch. It was just bizarre; something about a medical emergency in custody and a death. So, I called the shift supervisor to see if he needed help. He said the situation was crazy and that I shouldn't even think about going to the scene or anywhere near it. Well, of course, that just made me even more curious. So, I got out my laptop and looked up the call. You could tell just by reading the notes this was a mess — and turning into an even bigger mess."

"More and more people started gathering outside CUP Foods where the incident happened. I remember thinking, where's the command staff? Why weren't they doing anything? Why didn't they look up the call like I did and do something about it? I mean, even Chief Arradondo could have pulled up the call and realized there was a problem. They could've done something to prevent things from getting completely out of hand. But they didn't. And the chief, the assistant chief or any of the deputy chiefs were nowhere to be seen. The fact that they did nothing still bothers me to this day."

"I just got demoted, so maybe I had a different perspective. But everybody saw how Mayor Frey and Chief Arradondo gave in to ridiculous complaints — and just stood by while officers were getting cancelled and attacked. I don't know

---

46. Interview with Kim Voss, April 20, 2022.

when throwing somebody under the bus became an important part of leadership, but it did with Frey and Arradondo. For years, if something came up that made them look bad, they made it go away, or blamed somebody else for it. At the same time, if something made other people look bad, they just stepped aside and let them take the blame. But the hypocrisy never went away. I mean, we had 911 calls to Keith Ellison's house constantly and those got covered up—even when he beat up his girlfriend or fiancé or whoever she was at the time. His son Jeremiah got arrested for domestic violence and my office handled that one, too. Obviously, nothing happened with that case either. Jeremiah's on the city council and there's no mention of that anywhere. It's like it never happened. So that night, it seemed like the same lack of leadership showed up. Frey and Arradondo, and the rest of the command staff—they did nothing to prevent things from getting out of control with the riots. They just disappeared. They were absolutely horrible at preventing a bad situation from becoming worse. They'd always talk about organic leadership. That's something I'd put in my garden. But that's no excuse for failing to lead a city and a police department."

**Tuesday, May 26, 2020**

"The next night, Tuesday night, just proves my point. Things were already way out of control. When I would call the command post, there was nothing— crickets. There was just radio silence. Nobody answered and I never got a call back. Since nobody was telling us what to do, I figured I was self-deployed. I just did what I had to do. And nobody on the command staff had the nerve to stop me or say anything to me, partly because my officers respected me, and partly because they weren't even there. We were left floundering. So, I told everyone, it's just us out here. We've got to take care of ourselves because nobody is looking out for us. We had no backing from the city, no backing from the council. I don't think I even saw any of the top brass. Which is funny because they got all these accolades and praise for leadership during the riots, but I don't think I saw any of them doing anything to actually help. So, we—by that I mean everybody but the so-called command staff—we had to figure this out on our own. Myself, and the other lieutenants, along with the sergeants and beat cops did the best we could responding to 911 calls while dealing with the riots."

**Wednesday, May 27, 2020**

"The thing I remember most about Wednesday (May 27, 2020), was that we ran out of less-lethal ammunition that night. Again, we'd call the command post, and nobody would answer, or they'd answer and just hang up. There was no way to get anything that we needed. We had officers searching the backseats of patrol cars, old jacket pockets—we were scrounging around everywhere. With all the effort, we ended up with eight rounds of less-lethal, which was ridiculous. I remember thinking the whole time, how does this happen? How does a major metropolitan city run out of less-lethal ammunition? We couldn't protect ourselves or anybody else, but we did the best we could to make those eight rounds last through the night. In other words, we took a lot more damage than we should have."

**Thursday, May 28, 2020**

"The next morning, Thursday (May 28, 2020), I went to the precinct early, I wanted to talk to the sergeants on dogwatch (nightshift) and see how things were going. They said it was an absolute shit-show. They were getting hit with bottles and bricks, they were getting shot at—it was horrible what was happening to them. But everybody was going home in the upright position, and that's the most important thing. Then one of the sergeants said something I couldn't believe. I heard it, it happened, but I still can't believe it. One of the sergeants said we're 'giving up the precinct.' I didn't take it seriously—I mean, who gives up a precinct? But given everything else that was going on, I was curious to say the least. After the dogwatch guys left, I went to my office and started looking over cases for my investigators. Around nine or so, I heard the inspector came in—the inspector was in charge of the precinct, so I went down to talk to him. I started to ask about what the guys on dogwatch heard—but I didn't even finish before he flew off on me. He said I'm supposed to be a leader and had to put a stop to rumors, and it was my job to nip that kind of talk in the bud. At some point I told him, look, nobody is telling me *anything*, so I'm just asking you about what I heard. He went off repeating himself. At some point he finished his tirade, and I just went back upstairs to my office."

"Here's the part I still can't believe. About an hour later, the inspector sent somebody upstairs to tell me, 'Pack your stuff, we have to be out of here by two!' So, I get the reprimand for not stopping rumors. Then an hour later, somebody comes upstairs to tell me we're giving up the precinct!?" The command staff didn't think of telling me an hour ago? They had to send somebody else upstairs to tell me!? I didn't even have time to appreciate how ridiculous this was because I had to call my investigators and tell them to come in and pack up their stuff."

"When my investigators asked about what was going on, I had to tell them, 'Look, I don't know why, but you need to get all of your stuff out by two.' In the meantime, I grabbed a bunch of really big property bags, like oversize garbage bags, and started putting their names on it. Supposedly, the city was going to send over a truck or a bus or something and pick up everybody's stuff and bring it over to the SOC (Strategic Operations Center). While we were packing up, a city crew started putting up barriers and chain-link fencing outside the precinct. We had to pack up for about 30 or 40 people—then the command staff realized, we had the police museum downstairs, so we also had to take care of all that. We were in the middle of chaos, but apparently, we had plenty of time to waste packing up an entire precinct to sacrifice to the gods of left-wing cancel culture—the very people who started this whole mess. We got our stuff taken care of, but of course, the command staff forgot about the riot gear, police radios, and ammunition that were downstairs. In fact, some of the raid gear they left behind was stolen out of the precinct later that night."[47]

"None of this made any sense, and it was an absolute f-cking mess, so of course Mayor Frey had to be behind all of this. We had this same kind of thing happen before. It was a different mayor, but the same lack of leadership, same lack of a plan, and the same lack of communication. This was back in 2015 after the shooting of Jamar Clark. Mayor Hodges was dealing with the protestors who camped outside the fourth precinct for weeks. Mayor Hodges was as dumb as a box of f-cking rocks—and that's not being kind to the box or the rocks. I think Harteau, who was chief back then, said Betsy Hodges had great intentions but no abilities, or something like that."[48]

"That's probably the nicest thing a cop has ever said about Mayor Hodges. Back then, Hodges had a similar brilliant plan. Rather than deal with the actual situation, she wanted to just give up the fourth precinct, as if that would just make everything magically go away. At the time, I was appointed watch commander for the rest of the city, basically everywhere else but the precinct surrounded by protesters. I didn't have anything to do with their plans. But when I heard they were planning to give up the precinct, I wondered if anybody bothered to tell f-cked up Mayor Hodges that the fourth precinct housed the police firing range or that we kept guns and all of our ammunition

---

47. According to a press release issued on May 5, 2021 from the US Department of Justice, suspect Branden Michael Wolfe "entered the Third Precinct building and stole a police vest, duty belt, handcuffs, earpiece, baton, knife, riot helmet, pistol magazine, police radio, police overdose kit, uniform name plates, and ammunition. Wolfe was arrested on June 3, 2020, wearing the police vest, the duty belt and carrying the tactical baton." See also Raguse, L. (2021, May 5). St. Paul man sentenced, fined $12 million in Minneapolis Third Precinct fire. *KARE 11*.

48. *MPR News* quoted former Minneapolis police chief Janeé Harteau having said: "Oftentimes she had the best of intentions, but didn't have the ability"; Sepic, M. (2017, November 9). Police controversies, political missteps foiled Hodges in Minneapolis. *MPR News*.

in there? Hodges didn't know—the mayor had no idea what was in the fourth precinct or what she was about to give up. She had absolutely no clue."

"So now, here we are a few years later with history repeating itself. The names are different, back then it was Mayor Hodges, now it's Mayor Frey. But we're talking about the same kind of clueless people, trying to make themselves look good by feeding police officers to the wolves. As we started bringing everything out to the truck, the protesters were out there chanting and screaming, like they were since Tuesday. From the second the truck pulled up, they were on their phones videotaping the whole time. We were about done when I realized we still had an unmarked car in the lot. We already had a couple of police cars set on fire in the parking lot, so I found the keys and drove the unmarked to the SOC."

"When I got there, I asked the command staff, what's the plan? Again, nobody said anything. Then I mentioned, what about a Phase 3 callback? They didn't say anything. So, then I asked Henry Halvorson, one of the deputy chiefs, point blank, did you initiate a Phase 3 callback? He had absolutely no clue what I was talking about. He stared at me like a deer in the headlights. Anyway, we started calling everybody to work 12-hour shifts. They were going to send a bunch of officers back to the precinct. I was in uniform and ready to go, but Halvorson sent me home. He said I had been there long enough. This was around six o'clock on Thursday night. About two hours later, the precinct was gone. I was pissed. I should have been there to help. That was my precinct, that's where I was assigned. But I was sent home and I had to watch it burn on TV."

### Friday, May 29, 2020

"The next morning, I grabbed my camera and went down to the precinct. I didn't care if I had to kick the door in, or whatever was left of it. I was going to document everything that happened. It was still foggy inside from the sprinklers, which worked surprisingly. The windows had been busted out and I saw a city maintenance worker inside. I started talking to him through the broken window. I asked him how did they get through the barriers and the fencing? I said, it looked like they just pushed over the fence. He just started laughing. Then I asked him, seriously, how did they do that? He said, well, they didn't have time to secure the chain-link fencing to the barriers—so, yeah, anybody could've pushed it over—and that's what they did."

"Nobody cared to even do that right. It was like it was all for show. The protesters just pushed the fence over. Then they broke out the windows, and just like that, they were inside the precinct. But there were still 10 or 12 officers inside that night, along with some SWAT guys on the roof the whole time the 'peaceful protesters' were smashing out the windows and trying to burn it down. While I was walking around the building, I saw a few officers standing outside. They were ordered to take down the dedication plaque commemorating the year when the precinct was built. This made me sick, and it took me a while to go in because all I could do was cry. This wasn't just a building. It wasn't just where I worked—this was home. I finally got myself together and made my way upstairs. My office looked like it was hit by a Molotov cocktail or some kind of incendiary device. The other offices were torched, but mine was the only office that burned through. Maybe it was an easy target being right in the middle of the building. Who knows, but it was completely melted, there was absolutely nothing left in there. With the fake fencing, the officers taking down the plaque, and the precinct given up like that, I just fell apart. I was absolutely crushed. Nobody was looking out for us. So, I decided right then, that I'm just going to take care of my officers because nobody else was."

*A photo of a corner in Kim's office inside the Third Precinct taken while officers were evacuating on Thursday, May 28, 2020. Everything in the photo was left behind (Image provided by Dr. JC Chaix).*

*A photo of the same corner in Kim's office taken the next morning, Friday, May 29, 2020. Police leaders ordered officers to evacuate and abandon the Third Precinct. It was surrendered to rioters who then went inside, looted it, vandalized it, and then set it on fire (Image provided by Dr. JC Chaix).*

*(Top) Another photo of Kim's office taken Friday, May 29, 2020. (Bottom) Damage to the outside of the Third Precinct (Images provided by Dr. JC Chaix).*

*(Top) MPD SWAT officers on the roof of the Third Precinct during the second night of rioting, May 27, 2020 (Obtained and edited by Dr. JC Chaix). (Bottom) The aftermath of rioting on May 28, 2020 (Photo by Nick Peters Photography).*

## Saturday, May 30, 2020

"That Friday and Saturday night were just a blur. We did the best we could, although it didn't seem as hopeless as before now that we had help from other agencies with actual leaders. On Saturday night, sometime around three in the morning, we got a call from TCF Bank. People were breaking into the drive-thru window, probably to throw Molotov cocktails inside and burn it down. When we showed up, again seven squads deep, people started running. We jumped out, it seemed like every squad was in a foot chase. We ended up catching about seven suspects, so I called for transport. By now, about five days into all this, the command post might answer once in a while, but they still weren't doing anything.[49] When I called around, I found out Mike Kjos, the Assistant Chief, released the transport unit about two hours ago. I was like, are you f-cking kidding me!? Kjos, let the transport unit go home!? I mean, how do you release the transport unit in the middle of a riot? Apparently, arresting rioters and violent criminals wasn't a priority. We had to leave seven officers in the middle of a riot waiting around for someone to transport suspects."

## Taking Credit, Passing Blame

"As if morale couldn't be any worse, these officers were out there doing their jobs, risking their lives, chasing down the worst of the worst in the middle of the night. They did all of that just to be told 'Sorry, we don't have resources for you, we wanted to give the transport unit a break.' But seriously, they were taking care of other units, like transport, but they left the street cops to fend for themselves. Nothing could have been more demoralizing at that point, except for letting the world label and stereotype every MPD officer as a 'racist.' On

---

49. An audit report confirmed that Mayor Frey, Chief Arradondo, and the Minneapolis Police command staff failed to follow protocols and provide leadership; *City of Minneapolis: An after-action review of city agencies' responses to activities directly following George Floyd's death on May 25, 2020.* (2022, March 7). Hillard Heintze.

top of that, the street cops were the ones who had to smooth things over with citizens and anybody who called 911 for help. We apologized to practically everyone we met. We told them we were sorry about the rioting and the long delays, and that we were trying to make things right. I mean the citizens in our precinct; they were sleeping on their front porches armed with baseball bats, hunting rifles, or whatever they had to protect themselves. These people cared about their neighborhood. They would help us out. They would tell us, 'Hey, one ran that way' or 'one is hiding back there.' It was horrible. But then again, all of this was horrible."

## Leadership Priorities?

"A lot happened that week. On Saturday night, Assistant Chief Kjos called me and sounded very concerned. I thought he was going to tell me that we lost somebody. But instead, he was concerned because they just got a complaint that someone tried to vandalize the George Floyd memorial on 38th and Chicago. He wanted to know if I could send a car over there to handle the report. I could not believe what he was saying. I told him, 'We're a little busy at the moment with all the rioting.' We had four officers in seven squads running call, to call, to call along with absolute chaos going on around us. Kjos said something like, 'Well I don't need everybody to go, just one car.' Apparently, he was clueless, so I told him something like, 'Nobody is going anywhere alone. There are people out here trying to kill us, so we're sticking together and with all the calls backed up, I have no idea when we could get there even if we tried.' Kjos didn't say a word. It was awkward for a moment, but then he finally said he would just take care of it. I told him that's probably not a good idea, but he was too busy complaining to listen."

"If anything defined our leadership, and the lack of it, this was it. This would have been insane. In the middle of the riots, the MPD Assistant Chief wanted an officer to take a vandalism report at a memorial for someone who died in police custody—at the very spot where it happened—while surrounded by violent, armed, anti-police protesters during the worst rioting in the history of Minneapolis. If this doesn't show how clueless the command staff was, I don't know what does. But here's what made this the absolute worst of all: this was the only direct contact I had with the command staff during the riots. They never told us what to do. They never asked if we needed anything. I don't know what else to say, but we didn't have any leadership—they were too busy running around making excuses for themselves. The command staff abandoned us and stopped being leaders long before the riots broke out."

## Lies, Or the Final Straw

"Here's what got to me. If you're the chief or the mayor and you want to let a police precinct burn, that's fine. Politicians don't really have a clue. Letting a precinct burn down as an appeasement is fine, I guess—just as long as they know it's also a sign to the community that the police no longer care because that's what happened. People felt helpless. They were losing everything. Some were pissed when the Target store, the bank, the AutoZone, and everything else around the precinct burnt down. But they were even more pissed when they realized we had SWAT officers on the roof protecting the precinct. It looked like we weren't protecting them, but just protecting our building. That did not bode well in the community."

"Once again, police officers took the blame for that. But if someone would have asked me to get a group of officers together and go take back Target, AutoZone, or whatever, I would have done it in a heartbeat. Any officer would have done the same, but we couldn't. The command staff had no idea how those stores and everything else that burned down mattered to the people who lived here and mattered to us just the same. But we were told to just stand down and let it all happen. Every officer in that precinct was upset and frustrated about not being able to do anything."

"We had a chief who everybody thinks can walk on water, so of course he's perfect for playing a leading role in Mayor Frey's identity politics. The rest of us were just racist bastards, of course. That's to be expected these days. But what broke my back, was the lack of support, no direction, and now the blame. Meanwhile, we were put in a situation where we didn't know if we were going home at the end of the shift."

"For me, after 37 years of the bullshit and suffering that I've dealt with on this department, this wasn't just a job; it was my life. And most of the other officers, especially the ones who had been on a while, felt the same way. Nobody signs up to be a police officer because the pay is great, and the hours are perfect. You become a cop because you care, because you want to make a difference, and you want to make things better. And you don't sign up to stand down."

### Interview with Samantha Belcourt (Police Officer)

Kim wasn't the only Minneapolis police officer who suffered the lack of leadership during the riots. Officer Samantha "Sam" Belcourt also experienced the lies and hardships firsthand. Sam was part of a small team of police officers who were dispatched throughout the city during the riots. They rescued ambulance and fire crews, members of the National Guard, a truck driver surrounded by protesters, other police officers, and stabbing victims. Like a lot of Minneapolis cops, Sam was reluctant to talk about the riots. She didn't want to talk to the mainstream media because they made police officers the enemy. But now, more than two years later, she reached out to me to tell her story.

When I asked Sam about the most difficult thing she had to deal with, she paused for a moment. Then holding back, she said, "probably the hardest thing I had to do was turn in my resignation letter." She never wanted to quit. However, along with the hate and violence during the riots, the hate that continued long after rioters left the streets of Minneapolis eventually proved to be too much. Sam talked about some of the difficulties she endured.

"I absolutely loved going to work every day. There were plenty of opportunities to not only learn, but to help throughout the city. I also had the opportunity to do real police work. Here's just a small example; even if I got a call about a stolen bike, being able to drive around the neighborhood, find it, and bring it back felt good. It was rewarding and I felt like I was making a difference. That's what I liked about working for MPD, if you worked hard, they let you work hard, and I liked that. It was a great combination to have opportunities to make a difference with endless amounts of work to be done."

"That Tuesday (May 26, 2020), I was working days at the time with CRT (the Minneapolis PD Community Response Team). As I was leaving, my neighbor comes out and says, 'Hey, you know there was an incident last night. Somebody died in MPD custody, and it doesn't look good.' So, I said, 'Oh, OK, I didn't hear about it, but I'll check, I'll see what they have to say when I get into work.' When I went into work that morning, we pulled up the video—the cellphone video that pretty much everybody saw. We watched it... and we all just sat there... I was sick to my stomach because I knew this was bad. I don't know the full story, so I can't even comment—I still won't because I don't know the details. But I knew there was going to be a lot of anger, a lot of emotion, and a lot of hurt because of the video. I also knew it was probably going to be bad for us, for the police. We all kind of sensed nothing was going to be the same. There was just a tension. Everybody was nervous, even the veteran officers weren't sure about what was going to come from all of this."

"The CRT had access to the surveillance cameras throughout the city. So, we were watching the cameras and could see the floods of people coming in that day. People were mad and doing things like knocking over signs on the sidewalk. From just watching the cameras you could tell people were angry. That first night, two officers got trapped in their squad car near 38th and Chicago. They were dispatched to a call nearby and ended up getting surrounded by protesters and their car was getting damaged. A bunch of us went out there to help, but we couldn't even get within a couple of blocks of them because of all the people. We had to run through the crowd and try to get the officers out. We didn't have our helmets or anything, so we were getting pummeled with water bottles, rocks, pretty much anything the rioters could throw at us. We weren't trying to do crowd control. We just wanted to get those officers to safety, leave the area, and regroup. Fortunately, we did. After that, we kind of got the feeling that the protesters were moving to the Third Precinct. We also made our way over there. You could sense the anger and emotion feeding off itself."

"The directives we were given were basically, 'don't go there, just leave the Third Precinct be.' But we could tell listening to the radio that the officers inside the precinct were scared. We still weren't authorized to use tear gas, so we couldn't disperse the protesters away from the precinct. Then they started breaking the windows while officers were inside. It seemed like our commanders were taking a 'wait and see' approach. They were saying let the windows be broken, just leave the building. They were telling us to stand down—while officers inside the precinct were scared for their lives. We were outside trying to help. We were running through crowds, outnumbered by thousands, so I can only imagine how the officers trapped inside the precinct felt when the command staff was telling everybody to stand down while the rioters started breaking the windows and breaking down the doors."

"I've never been a part of a tactical briefing involving the 'wait and see' move, but that's what the command staff was doing. They abandoned the officers inside the building and were waiting to see what the protesters would do and how bad things would get. As someone with combat experience, I knew their approach wouldn't work. And it wasn't until the rioters almost breached the last door inside, before they authorized gas. After that, they allowed us to go in and rescue the officers."

"I think this is when it became personal for me. It's different to serve your country overseas. I didn't really have a connection or a sense of place there. This was a whole other feeling. Minneapolis wasn't just a place. I think people misunderstand the relationship police officers have with the city. I mean, oh my gosh, I spent more time there working or doing things on my days off than I ever did at home, not to mention all the overtime. We had good relationships with people, with the residents and business owners in different communities. This felt personal. There were officers who spent their whole adult lives in Minneapolis. Like the ones who joined when they were in their twenties and worked in the city for 30 years. Now, they're in their fifties, and had to watch the city they served get destroyed. It was just devastating."

"On top of that, the first night we were on the riot line outside the Third Precinct for about ten hours. It was pouring rain. We didn't have any protection, only our helmets and baton sticks, which were basically useless. Unfortunately, the Target store and Arby's had landscaping with these wonderful big rocks outside. Everybody across the street, maybe 25-30 yards away, had an endless supply of rocks to throw at the police. Myself, and my partners had tons and tons of bruises. They weren't life-threatening, but getting hit in the leg, the arm, the chest, or somewhere with a rock still hurts."

"It was painful to stand there and take that kind of physical abuse for 10 hours. Some officers were targeted more than others—one of my African American partners was targeted more than most. It was obvious because a lot of people were shooting pink paint-ball guns at officers and trying to hit them in the crotch, or the throat, or other vulnerable areas to cause some serious pain. It was sad to see your partners go through that. But they came back the next morning to defend the city with no complaints."

"The second night was worse. That's when the burning and looting started. We were assigned to escort firefighters. Burning buildings weren't necessarily a priority, but protecting lives and people were. As the riots moved down Lake Street, there were smaller businesses with residences above them. But it was just too dangerous for the fire department to go in there because people were destroying the firetrucks and attacking and assaulting the firefighters. They don't train to fight fires while fighting rioters. So, we were assigned to create a kind of barrier to keep the firefighters as safe as possible."

"I'm not sure if other teams were assigned to do the same thing, but we escorted firefighters into the parking lot of the AutoZone store, which was burning right across from the Third Precinct. There were chemicals involved in that fire, it was just awful, and my lungs hurt for weeks afterwards because the air was so bad. Although just as bad, rioters were attacking the police and fire vehicles. We were outnumbered, tires were getting stabbed, and mirrors were getting blown off. We did all we could to create space between the rioters and the firefighters. Even just a little bit helped keep them safe. While my partner and I were on foot, we noticed people inside the new apartment building that was being built next to the AutoZone. It was a huge wooden structure. And for about an hour and a half, we watched protesters build a perfect bonfire—but all we could do is watch."

*Officer Belcourt watched rioters light a bonfire inside a 190-unit apartment building under construction on May 27, 2020. Since officers could not make arrests, the building turned into an inferno (Source: SingleSpeakMedia).*

"We didn't have the resources to stop them or the authorization to arrest them. When the fire chief arrived on scene, we pointed out the bonfire, thinking maybe they would throw water on the apartment building or try to make it harder for them to burn it down. But he said, 'Nope, we've got other priorities,' or something like that. Nobody was living there, so they had to save their resources for places where people lived instead."

"Speaking of places where people lived and worked, on the third day we had a late morning briefing. We were told to get our personal effects out of the Third Precinct since they're giving it up as a prize. We all laughed—it was the dumbest thing we ever heard. It made no sense tactically, and no sense whatsoever. We had been dealing with everything for two and a half days at this point. We knew that giving them the precinct wasn't going to achieve anything. We thought someone on the command staff had an inkling to know better. We honestly laughed it off—but it turned out to be the biggest mistake and a waste of millions of taxpayer dollars."

"Before they gave up the Third Precinct, there were thousands of people around it. By now, they had three days to kind of claim that territory. AutoZone burned down and the Target store had already been looted. I can't remember the exact time that day, but we got a call about a stabbing in the middle of the crowd. They were trying to verify the legitimacy of the call, because they weren't going to dispatch officers, firefighters, or an ambulance into all of this to be victimized. It ended up that two people were stabbed. There was also the suspect with a knife—and a concerned citizen with a concealed-carry permit holding the suspect at gunpoint. Protesters were moving in to hurt the suspect, so the fire department and the ambulance couldn't get through. One of the bigger problems was that when protesters saw law enforcement coming, they just assumed we were coming in for an arrest, but we were coming in to help."

"After dealing with all that, it was just another day—endless hours of basically losing everywhere we went. I hate to say it like that because it's not about winning or losing, but we were losing when it came to helping people. To drive around and see shops destroyed and business owners bawling their eyes out; I just wanted to give them a hug and tell them that I was sorry. But there was nothing we could do, and that felt like losing. Giving up the precinct was almost like putting up the white flag, like we surrendered saying, 'Here ya go, we give up!' I know that's how police officers felt, so I can imagine other people felt the same way."

"This didn't end when the riots ended. People were still being violent toward each other and the police. A few weeks after the riots, we were working a detail downtown, and found a guy lying on the street. So, we jumped out to help him. He'd been shot in the chest. We're trying to render aid to him. Once again, protesters start closing in on us. They get angry and we're getting stuff thrown at us, while I've basically got my fingers inside his chest trying to stop the bleeding. More officers rushed in to help and escort the ambulance. The crowd was angry and calling us names, and nobody was giving us any information about what happened. It felt like a lose-lose battle because while we're plugging a hole in this guy's chest, he starts calling us names too. If he was in any better shape, he would've told us to get lost. It was like, OK, the riots are over, but not really over, because people still just hated us. We'd be driving along patrolling a street and people would throw things at us, and you're left wondering what the heck just happened?"

"All of that just kind of compiles inside you, it builds up. At some point, you have to question 'Is this for me, am I going to be good enough to do this job— and is this job good enough for me?' As a cop, there's going to be side effects to all the feelings and things you experience, and it's going to affect your personal life. I didn't want my personal life to be negatively affected by my job. It was just too much. Even before the riots, you'd drive around and have memories—someone was shot over there, we arrested a homicide suspect right here, we had a suicidal person jump off that building over there—all the traumatic situations that officers deal with on a regular basis. There's so much of it, especially since only about five percent of what happens gets reported on the news. I remember before the riots when we had multiple shootings downtown and you didn't see any of that on the news. You didn't hear a peep on the news when people were dropping like flies when the bars would close at night. Whether it was reported or not, you need time to heal from that. After the riots, there wasn't any time to heal physically or mentally. So, I took some time off. But then, it wasn't just the idea of going back to work, even just checking an email wasn't happening and didn't feel right. So that's when I had to accept ending my career in law enforcement."

"But I think the worst is how I feel about my fellow officers who are still hanging in there—I mean honestly clinging on for dear life, because they don't have the option to move on. Imagine you have a two-year law enforcement degree, you have three small children, you're the main income earner for the house with full insurance. Where are you going to go and make the same income with the same benefits? So, a lot of officers are just hanging on and trying to do their absolute best because they have to take care of their families. But a lot of them are just stuck and they're just sucking it up."

"I think a lot of people forget that we're human beings, we're not just a uniform. Even though it's a career, you put passion, energy, and part of yourself into being a police officer probably more than any other job. So, imagine how it feels when one person, say someone in the accounting department of a big company, someone you don't know or never met, steals money from the company. That's bad enough but imagine if the company doesn't just blame that person, but they blame everybody and say, 'You're all horrible. In fact, if we could legally fire all of you, we would, because we don't want any of you here. Since we can't fire you, we're going to make things miserable, and make you all work 20-hour shifts until you burn yourselves out.' That's basically what happened to most of us at MPD."

"Imagine if a friend told you this was their work environment. What would you tell them? That is, after asking them things like, 'Why are you still working there? Why would you keep working in that environment?' So, one of the hardest things I ever did was send my resignation letter. I worked so hard for my job. But when you feel like you can't do it anymore—or you feel like you're not wanted—it's hard to go on."

(Top) Minneapolis police officers on Lake Street near the Third Precinct being hit with rocks and bottles, as Sam Belcourt mentioned (public domain photo). (Bottom) Some of the anti-police graffiti that appeared overnight throughout the city (Photo by Nick Peters Photography).

*(Top) Inside one of the many stores that were looted during the riots. (Bottom) What was left of buildings and cars that were set on fire during the riots (Photos by Nick Peters Photography).*

**Interview with Scott Creighton (Police Officer)—Part I**

Along with Kim and Sam, officer Scott Creighton also spoke about his experiences. Scott was injured during the riots but kept working afterward. But the lack of leadership eventually led him to question himself and his sacrifices. After dealing with two shootings, a "man with a gun" call, and not being able to find a supervisor anywhere, he realized that after 28 years, he could no longer serve the city he loved without any support. Incidentally, Scott arrested George Floyd in 2019—about a year before Floyd was arrested and died in 2020. Here's what Scott recalled when asked about his career with MPD, the riots, and arresting George Floyd during an undercover drug operation…

"My family was from Minneapolis. My grandfather was a fireman, my dad was a cop for nearly 40 years. My father-in-law was a cop. My family was service-oriented. So, with my background and having been in the military, there was no question about what I would be doing for a living. But everything with the riots changed my perspective."

"But first I should say that the Jamar Clark shooting in 2015 was like a prelude to the riots in 2020. At least, I believe the situation should never have happened under that administration, and the riots shouldn't have happened under this one. But here's the thing, back then Arradondo was a lieutenant, and in 2020 he was the chief. So, there's a connection there. He was a good guy and all. He'd give you a pat on the back and say, 'Good job' and all that. But he didn't get into anything. Most of the time he was a ghost."

"So, when I look back at what happened with the Clark shooting, I know why the riots happened. He just wasn't a leader. He's a nice guy, but *not* a leader. I mean back then, I was there. I was a part of that. The protesters had us surrounded after the Jamar Clark shooting. They occupied the street. We couldn't leave the precinct for days and that whole thing lasted more than two weeks. We had the mayor, Chief Harteau, and our inspector—they lied to us about what was going on. I mean our inspector was lying just to keep his job. It was awful, and nothing but appeasements."

"After the Jamar Clark situation, we told them, 'Hey, you've got to be prepared for something like this, because next time, things might not work out. But they didn't want to hear anything about it. They didn't do any planning for it; they didn't do any kind of training for it—they didn't do a thing about it. It was like well that happened, it's over, it's done with. They left us stranded with the Clark incident, and they did the same again in 2020. But this time, they didn't just occupy a precinct, they took over the whole city. They didn't realize we were outnumbered until it was too late. The first day they did nothing. They did nothing the second day. By the third day, it was too late. They were trying to plug the dam after the flood."

"That Tuesday, the first day (May 26, 2020) we were assigned to the alley and the back parking lot. My unit was the CRT team, so we went out whenever there was a critical incident. We weren't 911 and we didn't go to calls for service. We were like 'para-SWAT' in a way, or at least that's what I would call it. Whenever there were riots and stuff like that, they'd put us with SWAT."

"People started gathering outside the Third Precinct because that's where Chauvin was assigned. That morning, the crowd was maybe only about 200 hundred people or so. They weren't out front and didn't take over Lake Street yet. They had us set up in line formation up against a wall. For what it was, it seemed kind of OK at first. But then sometime later that afternoon—out of the blue they just start throwing rocks and bottles and everything. Next thing you know, they're throwing stuff over the buildings at us. What happened to me was this. We were standing with our backs against the wall. Somebody threw a brick and it bounced off the wall and hit me in the jaw. It broke three of my teeth. It also broke a bridge I had because that was loose. I ended up having seven teeth taken out. It was a bit worse than I thought and took about 16 months to fix everything. But that happened on the first day. My partner— same thing, she got her teeth broken. I mean we were looking out, but once things started coming over the buildings and bouncing off the walls behind us, there wasn't much we could do. It was like a rain of bricks. We didn't even see it coming. We got hit. But we were there the next day."

"That second day there were two critical incidents that happened, but with all the lawsuits, I don't know if I should talk about any of that. But there were two incidents that day, and I'm not sure if they ever told the media or the public about both. The first one we went to; someone was stabbed outside the Target parking lot. She was on the phone with 911, and they were trying to get us to her. Then we find out somebody else was stabbed. So, we had to get them out, too. We also had the suspect with a knife and a gun. In the middle of all that chaos, people were throwing things at us. It was the scariest situation I've ever been in throughout my entire life. We were surrounded by thousands of people."

"The part that really got to me was that once we went in to help, the protesters started closing in behind us. So, we had no way out. We had to get through barricades to get in there, and then they closed the barricades behind us. We had to bust our way in and then bust our way out of there. Anyway, we got the suspect and the first victim out. We saved the second one too, initially. I mean, we got her out of there—we got her to the ambulance, which was staging over by the city garage on Hiawatha and 24th. They got her stabilized. But she died later that night in the hospital. I don't think anyone has ever reported about that.[50] The administration never said anything about it. That's probably

---

50. Both Scott and Sam were involved in the rescue of two victims during this incident. The second victim who presumably died at the hospital, is not mentioned in after-action reports. See: Nine News Australia. (2020, May 28). *Minneapolis protests erupt on camera after man allegedly stabbed* [Video]. YouTube.

because this was all supposed to be a *peaceful* protest. They didn't even consider it to be a critical incident."

"After that night, we were assigned back to the Third Precinct. The state troopers were there, but they were told to stage. That night, I got hit with a frozen bottle. That's another thing—they wouldn't let us wear protective gear. It was a riot, but they only let us wear our helmets. I mean, we had all the gear with us, but they thought it was too offensive and military-like. I got pelted with rocks all over my body because they—the administration—they couldn't make a decision for nothing. We had very weak leaders and their decision-making was worse. I know most of them. They never really worked the street, so their experience was limited. They were good people, good managers, but they weren't good leaders. And we all suffered because of that. So, when this all started happening, none of them knew what to do. The other thing, which was a big problem, they always tried to defer or downplay everything. It was as if things were never as bad as they were. They were just ignoring the truth."

"That's why I quit. After the riots, after getting hurt, and all the bullshit, all the stuff I saw happen, and how it affected other officers and everyone else in the city, it was like everything I loved was destroyed. In one way or another it all got destroyed. I was so frustrated. I tried to go to the administration—one of my best friends was a deputy chief. I mean, Halvorson and I, we lived together for two years when we first joined the department. But now, he'd didn't know anything. He didn't even know I got injured, he had no idea what I was talking about. I tried to reach out to him, but he didn't even have the time of day for me. I've known him for 30 years. But now he was just acting like the rest of the administration. He didn't want to hear anything. That's because anything that was wrong, made them look bad."

"After the riots, and with COVID and all that, a lot of officers were starting to leave the department. I was still working the streets in a CRT unit, which meant you went out and looked for stuff, people committing crimes. But the way the policies were being re-written and everything else, people were just staying inside waiting for calls. I can't compare to my dad; he was a legend on the department. But like him, I was out there rolling around by myself. There'd be shootings, shots fired, stabbings and I'm out there by myself. There were shootings every day. On my last day, I went out, two people got shot here, three people got shot over there. Then I get a 'guy with a gun' call. I'm like two blocks away. I see the suspect walking down an alley with a handgun. I'm waiting for backup... Nothing... Still nothing... So, I go in the alley. I do my job. Then afterward I started thinking about it. I realize this isn't worth it anymore. No matter what I did, or how it turned out, it was going to be used against me. It was going to be a no-win situation. If he started shooting at me, and I died, well that wouldn't end well. And if I start shooting at him, I could be the next Derek Chauvin."

"I stopped and asked myself, 'What am I doing?' Years ago, in my fifth year on the job I got severely injured. I almost lost my eye and had 17 surgeries. Between that, my teeth, the riots—everything I gave to this department—and then I get no backing? That same week, I went in to find my sergeant, he wasn't there. I looked around for my lieutenant, he wasn't there. I go to find a street sergeant; nobody has seen any of them. There was no inspector. No lieutenants. I went down to city hall to find somebody or talk to somebody about this. But all of city hall was like a ghost town. There was nobody there— no administration—nobody. I'm still trying to do my job every day, getting hurt, risking my life—and where is everybody else? I mean, what more can I give to this city, to this administration for absolutely nothing in return?"

## Interview with Gary Nelson (SWAT Team Commander)

The way Minneapolis Police officers were treated doesn't say much for leadership. It also doesn't say much for the hope and future of Minneapolis. It seemed clear that the police command staff, Chief Arradondo, and Mayor Frey were hardly the strong leaders they claimed to be. About the only thing positive to say was that they were consistent. They consistently failed the department and city before, during, and after the riots. Like Scott, Sam, and Kim, many MPD officers were willing to give the benefit of the doubt and support for their leaders at first. The riots were unlike anything anyone on the department had ever dealt with before. But as the days and weeks went by, the lack of leadership became even more of a catastrophic failure not only for the police department but for everyone in the city of Minneapolis.

Lieutenant Gary Nelson was a SWAT team commander and assigned to the Third Precinct. He was defending it when city leaders decided to surrender it. Despite the horror of being on the roof when protesters were setting it on fire, Gary initially thought it was best to overlook the failures, fall in line, and show support to move forward. He even did so publicly, thinking that aside from the long overdue "Told ya so" moment, that Frey and Arradondo would finally listen and take planning and riot response seriously.

Gary soon realized they had no real interest in learning from their mistakes. When they started blaming everybody else for their epic failures, Gary couldn't bear the hypocrisy, especially since he tried to warn the command staff that they needed better planning and training to deal with riots and other civil disturbances. Six months *before* the riots, Gary had sent an email to the command staff. It included a proposal for a "Mobile Field Force," a way to help MPD be better prepared for riots, demonstrations, and other large-scale events. Gary also mentioned the necessary training that could start as early as January 2020.

# Mobile Field Force Proposal

## Nelson, Gary (Police)
Tue 11/26/2019 6:24 PM

To:      Gerlicher, Scott
Cc:      Waite, Kathy; Kjos, Michael; Blackwell, Katie M.; Mercil, Johnny

Forwarded on 11/28/2019 6:20 AM
MPD MFF Proposal.docx (56 KB)

Commander Gerlicher,

I have been thinking a lot about the conversation that we all had during the AAR related to the past MAGA Rally, the desire for Civil Disturbance/ MFF training in the near future, and the possible consideration of creating a MFF as a secondary assignment. Please find the attached Mobile Filed Force (MFF) Proposal which I believe would expand our capabilities in the area of Civil Disturbance response, both from an OPERATIONS lens as well as a TRAINING lens (both in-service and pre-service). I know that the contemplation of forming a MFF as a secondary assignment is a different conversation from the anticipated Civil Disturbance/ MFF training being planned for next year, starting as early as January, but from a training sustainably perspective they are related under this proposal. This proposal is forward thinking and would give us capabilities in the response to civil disturbance that we currently either do not have or struggle to achieve in situations where we it. I have highlighted in yellow the areas in the proposal that would address training capabilities moving into the future.

Best Regards,

Lieutenant Gary Nelson
Minneapolis Police Department
Special Operations

MPD MFF Proposal- FINAL.docx 52.59 KB

---

*Email sent by Lt. Gary Nelson to Commander Scott Gerlicher (and Deputy Chief Kathy Waite, Assistant Chief Mike Kjos, Commander Katie Blackwell, and Lt. Johny Mercil) regarding a proposal for Mobile Field Force to better prepare MPD for riots, demonstrations, and related civil disturbances. Nelson sent his proposal on November 28, 2019, six months before the riots (Email obtained and provided by Dr. JC Chaix).*

---

### MPD Mobile Field Force Proposal

**END GOAL:** *Interagency collaboration would be the ultimate end goal; a metro-wide MFF that could come together to provide a control force of approximately 300 officers in the unlikely event that such a response force is warranted. This partnership would allow for improved interagency relationships along with consistency and continuity related to the type of training and response capabilities across all participating agencies to ensure a high level of interoperability. Recommended best practices assert that now is the time to draft a robust Mutual Aid Deployment and Coordination Plan specific to civil disturbance events. A metro-wide MFF would conduct a training exercise annually to ensure tactics and method are consistent. There is a real opportunity here to develop a robust metro-wide CD response plan for large scale or expanded civil disturbance events through partnerships with other large metro agencies to include the MN State Patrol.*

*In closing, I want to reiterate that the authorization of a Mobile Field Force, as a secondary assignment/unit, would give us the following two (2) capabilities that we currently do not have.*

1. *Allow for a readily trained and equipped group of officers to respond on short notice to a situation where MFF response is necessary and required (**Operational Capability**).*

2. *Provide for a cadre of trained individuals and subject matter experts to support the MPD and the MPD Training Unit in conducting pre-service and periodic in-service Civil Disturbance and MFF training that is in accordance with the National standards and recommended best practices outlined in training developed by the Department of Homeland Security and FEMA. (**Training Capability**).*

---

*Page 5 of Lt. Nelson's proposal pointing out the need for interagency collaboration, better response capabilities, and training sent to MPD leaders on November 28, 2019—which again, he sent six months before the riots (Email obtained and provided by Dr. JC Chaix).*

Gary's proposal would have made a difference during the riots, but it was basically ignored. That's probably because it didn't fit any of the top-level priorities. Frey and Arradondo seemed far more concerned with their reputations and appearances than protecting citizens and police officers. Unfortunately, they didn't take his proposal seriously. Gary explained how they just kept ignoring reality and pointing fingers...

"MPD policy regarding civil control was a joke. Nobody wanted to own what happened during the riots. They had plenty of chances to make decisions and be prepared. Instead, it was like deliberate indifference—they simply chose not to do anything. They knew better, but they did nothing to make things better. Being prepared wasn't something they cared about. If this were a football game, it wasn't like the coach made a bad call and the team lost. It's like the coaches didn't even show up! They weren't on the field! They weren't even there! I saw Frey and Arradondo once during the riots—once! That was it."

"As far as making bad calls, that's all they did during the rare moments they were around. Calling for mutual aid, getting the state troopers and the National Guard was a joke. They did nothing right. It would take months before all of this would come to light. There was a report that talked about all the failures in detail.[51] But what happened after that? Nothing. Arradondo stayed on, Frey was re-elected, so nothing changed. At first, I thought there'd be meaningful changes. I even signed an open letter supporting all of that.[52] But a week later I resigned. The city leaders wrecked this department and the city of Minneapolis. And nothing was going to be fixed anytime soon. It still haunts me to this day because I just don't understand why they let it all happen. With the riots, people were seriously injured, a police station was destroyed, livelihoods were lost. But the only ones held accountable were the officers and first-line supervisors who were sent out into a war zone ill-equipped and ill-prepared and told to stop the rioting. They were set up to fail by everyone in the chief's office—they're the ones who decided not to be prepared, but they were never held responsible or accountable for any of it."

---

51. Gary was referring to the following: Review of lawlessness and government responses to Minnesota's 2020 Riots. (2020, October 8). *Joint Transportation and Judiciary and Public Safety Committee Minnesota Senate.*

52. Olson, R. (2020, June 12). Minneapolis police officers issue open letter condemning colleague in George Floyd's death, pledging to work toward trust. *Star Tribune.*

civil unrest in Minneapolis was unprecedented; however, the lack of a basic crisis response framework was evident and limited the MPD's ability to respond appropriately. As indicated, simply identifying and designating individuals to the command post in advance increases initial response effectiveness and leads to a more comprehensive, confident and efficient crisis response.

Field personnel who we interviewed felt that in the first two days of the protest and unrest, MPD leadership, and presumably the City, attempted to keep the incident low profile and did not request additional resources, such as using callback or requesting assistance from other agencies. Further, officers stated that officers and agencies offered help and MPD leadership declined the offers. As a result, officers lost faith and trust in leadership.

### Field Response and Tactics

Absent a field force or specific cadre of officers trained in crowd control, the MPD assigned strike teams for incident response designated from MPD's Community Response Team, a plainclothes street crimes unit. This unit is composed of 10 officers who typically walk a beat and one sergeant. The unit works closely together daily. Many of these officers were former SWAT members and have tactical training, a higher level of training than patrol officers.

Staff in the command post called on these teams as needed and pulled officers from the various precincts to create additional strike teams. The precinct officers may or may not have had any specialized training, such as in crowd-control tactics. The command post staff located protective gear for the strike teams from equipment leftover from the Republican National Convention 12 years earlier. The equipment and some shields were issued to the strike teams for civil unrest protection.

The strike teams had squad cars and worked anywhere from 12 to 18 hours per day, staging at the convention center. Typically, by 1 or 2 p.m., the teams were actively engaged with violent individuals. A chemical agent response team (CART) supported the strike team officers. Several interviewees stated that the teams were very active. Incident Command staff dispatched teams to reports of violent behavior, engaged the groups to disperse the crowds and then retreated. MPD leadership stated that they simply did not have enough adequate resources to try any other tactic. They were strictly defensive and reactionary.

Once the MNG and the Minnesota State Patrol arrived in force, they partnered with the MPD and other assisting agencies, such as the Hennepin County Sheriff's Office, to address agitators in the larger groups. With the additional personnel, the teams took on a targeted approach and, with the help of an established curfew, began to see some success in decreasing the violence while preserving protesters' First Amendment rights.

*Some of the same things Lt. Nelson warned about in his email, before the riots, were coincidentally highlighted as failures of city leaders during the riots (Source: City of Minneapolis: An after-action review of city agencies' responses to activities directly following George Floyd's death on May 25, 2020. (2022, March 7). Hillard Heintze.*

## Hoping for a Cop to Get Hurt

Another high-ranking MPD supervisor, who wished to remain anonymous, [53] said that even if you could forget the rioting and the destruction, there was one thing that showed the disturbing priorities of city leaders:

"It was like they wanted a cop to get shot—not killed, just shot. Giving up the precinct was a show, like if the protesters could claim victory, this would all just go away. But Frey made his priorities obvious. When they were getting all the stuff out of the Third Precinct, a bus pulled right up to the back door. That was for all the property. But when they evacuated the people, it was parked blocks away. The property was safe and taken care of, but not the cops. They had to run through a violent crowd of thousands of people. This wasn't just shame and embarrassment. They had to run through a violent mob and everything they threw at them to a get to a bus that was blocks away. This wasn't about protecting officers. This was a deliberate move to put them in danger. Who does that? Who would make officers suffer like that?"

In hindsight, it seems like Frey, Arradondo, and the city council wanted the police to be outnumbered, as if letting looters and rioters have their way with the city was a reparation of some kind. As part of that, it seemed that giving up the precinct was an appeasement—and possibly even a planned ambush. The city council seemed to be exploiting the riots to advance their agenda to defund and dismantle the MPD.[54] One of their members was clearly demanding police officers to stand down and surrender the precinct. Council member Jeremiah Ellison, the son of Attorney General Keith Ellison, said as much during a live interview with Minnesota Public Radio (MPR) just hours before the precinct was given up and officers faced an unimaginable situation.

---

53. Identity withheld (personal communication, April 21, 2022).

54. Fletcher, S. (2020, June 5). I'm a Minneapolis City Council member. We must disband the police—Here's what could come next. *Time*; Casiano, L. (2020, June 4). Minneapolis City Council President, dem Jeremiah Ellison claim they'll 'dismantle' police. *Fox News*.

Like father, like son, Jeremiah also officially declared his support for Antifa. So, it's not surprising that he demanded MPD officers to "sacrifice" the Third Precinct—and not scare protesters:[55]

> "Take out everything important or dangerous... And you say, 'Look, we're not going to stand with our really scary-looking rifles and face masks and act like we're in opposition to a group of people who, as of last night, were scared and righteously angry.'"

Maybe in some political fantasy land that might work. But the lack of leadership turned the situation into an absolute nightmare.

### "In Case I Don't Make It..."

Another officer was inside the Third Precinct the night it was abandoned and burned. After rioters began attacking the building, the officer started writing a letter—it was meant to be a last "goodbye" for the officer's family. The Third Precinct didn't make it through the night, but fortunately, the officer survived. The next morning, after witnessing the devastating failure of police and city leaders, the officer finished the letter and sent it to Bob and the police union. The officer wanted the letter to remain anonymous out of fear of retaliation. Out of respect for the officer and the officer's family, only parts of the letter have been edited and included here.

"We got to the station around 16:00 hours. We were given orders to hold the precinct. I secured all the doors with zip-ties and extension cords. We were doing everything we could. But the supervisors weren't making any plans for a hostile takeover. There was no rally point, no contingency plans—nothing. I tried talking to the supervisors, but they weren't listening. So, I helped other officers bring food, water, fire extinguishers, and other supplies to the second

---

55. Caputo, A., Craft, W., & Gilbert, C. (2020, June 3). 'The precinct is on fire': What happened at Minneapolis' 3rd Precinct—and what it means," *MPR News*.

floor. If rioters broke in, we were going to barricade ourselves up there. After setting up on the second floor, we went to the third floor, closed all the blinds, and moved tables and chairs away from the windows. Then we went up to the roof. We stayed there for a couple of hours and watched as the crowd grew more hostile."

"At some point, we were ordered inside and told to stay out of sight. A group of rioters breached the front gate outside the precinct. A team of officers went out and secured it with zip-ties because that's all we had. Another group attacked the south end of the precinct to try and block us inside. Around 21:30, 21:45, a much larger group of rioters began to form in a nearby parking lot. All of us were ordered to the roll-call room. That's when the supervisors told us to abandon the precinct. They did a quick headcount and told us that a bus was en route to pick us up. The bus wasn't coming to the back parking lot; we were going to have to run to meet the bus about half a mile away. I'm guessing, an hour later or so, we started running out. We couldn't get the gate open because the protesters blocked us in. Officers got in a squad car and rammed the gate open."

"Almost as soon as we started running, the crowd started yelling, "Get them!" They were throwing heavy rocks at us and anything else they had. They were attacking and surrounding us. At one point we fired a stinger ball to keep them from getting any closer. We finally made it to the meeting point, just south of 32nd Street on Hiawatha. But the bus was late. We just stood there, surrounded by an angry mob closing in on us. Every minute felt like an hour until the bus finally arrived."

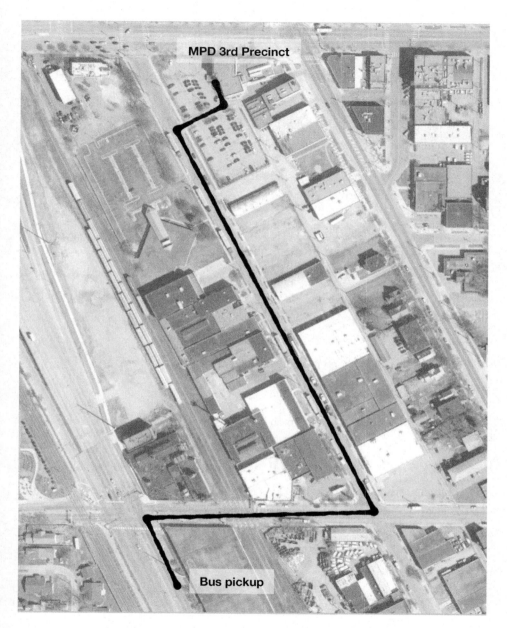

*The route that officers took from the 3rd Precinct to a bus pickup area while running through the crowd of rioters. It was approximately half a mile (Map source: MapIT Minneapolis).*

## Blaming Cops for all the Blame

Surviving that situation was bad enough. But other city council members seized the opportunity to blame cops because they didn't just give up the precinct. It seems like they were trying to push a narrative that cops were just defending themselves and doing nothing for the citizens of Minneapolis. For example, city council member Andrew Johnson told the media:[56]

> "It looked like they were defending the Alamo and letting the community burn."

This was just one of the many political insults hurled at MPD officers, many of whom were injured physically and emotionally and left to cope without any support from the command staff and city leaders. As Sam explained, it seemed like they were following a strategic plan; something like, if we can't fire them, we'll make them miserable until they quit. But when things became so unbearable, even quitting was an impossible challenge. Like when Scott finally had enough, he couldn't even quit because the supervisors and so-called leaders were nowhere to be found.

While officers were left to fend for themselves and try to make sense of it all, the media and the Left kept reinforcing a misleading narrative. They were leading people to believe that all of this was justified because of "systemic police racism." The insanity on social media certainly didn't help anyone think for themselves. Any difference of opinion didn't stand a chance—along with the facts and findings of George Floyd's official autopsy report.

---

56. Caputo, A., Craft, W., & Gilbert, C. (2020, June 30). 'The precinct is on fire': What happened at Minneapolis' 3rd precinct—and what it means. *MPR News.*

# PART III

## THE AUTOPSY &
## THE POINT OF NO RETURN

## The Autopsy Report/Review

The release of George Floyd's official autopsy report marked a point of no return. The report clearly indicated that Floyd did not have any life-threatening injuries—and died from cardiac arrest. This could have been caused by several factors including two significant heart diseases and the combination of fentanyl, methamphetamine, and THC in his system. With all that in mind, there's plenty of reason to doubt that George Floyd died because a "white police officer" was "crushing his neck into the pavement."

The autopsy conducted by the Hennepin County Medical Examiner forced the media, the Left, and everybody else to make a tough decision. They could either admit they jumped to conclusions; or they could insist they were right and lie about it all. Although, with the firestorm of self-righteousness and identity politics, nobody was about to admit they were wrong about anything. Even the most honest people among us seemed to be thinking twice out of fear of embarrassment and getting ripped apart by cancel-culture vultures.

The official autopsy of George Floyd was conducted 12 hours after he died. Just to be clear, the autopsy was conducted before the rioting and the looting started. So, it's difficult to ignore how someone could've spoken up about the preliminary findings and done something to help prevent the misperceptions and violence. However, the autopsy report wasn't released until a week later. That is, the report wasn't released until after all four officers were fired without due process, after former officer Derek Chauvin was arrested for third-degree murder and second-degree manslaughter, and block after block of Minneapolis was left in ruins.

Things were a bit more complicated because two conflicting reports were released about the same time. One was the official autopsy report from the Hennepin County Medical Examiner, which was based upon an actual autopsy examination and toxicology results. The other was a review from doctors hired by the family of George Floyd to offer their opinions about the viral Facebook video. In other words, they paid two doctors to say exactly what they wanted to hear about his death.[57]

### The Official Autopsy Report

The official autopsy report from the Hennepin County Medical Examiner's Office contradicted just about everything the media and the Left *assumed* about the death of George Floyd. Even *Newsweek* pointed it out:[58]

> "The preliminary findings in the Hennepin County Medical Examiner's autopsy of Floyd 'revealed no physical findings that support a diagnosis of traumatic asphyxia or strangulation.'"

The article also explained a significant fact that many overlooked:

> "George Floyd could not breathe prior to his restraint, prompting legal speculation that the charges against him may not hold up in court."

The official autopsy report proved that the accusations based on the viral video were likely all wrong. It also proved that the demands for "justice" were mistaken. George Floyd couldn't have died from his neck getting "crushed" by Derek Chauvin's knee because there were no signs of "traumatic asphyxia or strangulation" or other life-threatening injuries to his neck or throat. The autopsy report also undermines the narrative that George Floyd, a Black man, was murdered by a racist White police officer. There's little doubt that Floyd stopped breathing. But as the title of the autopsy report indicates, George Floyd died from "cardiopulmonary arrest" —his heart suddenly stopped and so did his breathing while he was in police custody. There were also other

---

57. Robles, F., & Burch, A. D. (2020, June 2). How did George Floyd die? Here's what we know," *The New York Times*.

58. Fearnow, B. (2020, May 30). George Floyd couldn't breathe before he was pinned down by cops, prosecutor says. *Newsweek*; emphasis added.

findings that seemed to disappear or were changed without much explanation after the fact. Just hours after completing the autopsy, Dr. Baker met with two Hennepin County attorneys, two special agents from the BCA, and four FBI agents and shared his preliminary findings with them. Once his findings were made known, Dr. Baker said several current and former medical examiners and other professionals reached out to him. Shortly afterward, his office received hundreds of death threats and threatening phone calls. Dr. Baker later testified that the revisions he made to his initial findings were his own and not the result of any outside influence.[59]

However, during a grand jury hearing in February 2021,[60] when a federal prosecutor asked Dr. Baker if he had been threatened, Dr. Baker said he needed to speak with his attorney. After consulting with his attorney about a basic yes or no question for about two hours, Dr. Baker returned to the stand: "No" was his answer.[61] None of this was typical, and a lot of it was questionable. Despite the evidence, the media and the Left weren't about to accept the findings of the official autopsy report. Doing so, would've required them to admit they were wrong, which would've meant that "peaceful protesters" burned down Minneapolis for nothing more than misperceptions.

---

59. Forliti, A., Karnowski, S., & Webber, T. (2022, February 1). Medical examiner: No pressure on Floyd autopsy report. *AP News.*

60. Balsamo, M. (2021, February 24). Federal grand jury hearing evidence in death of George Floyd. *ABC News.*

61. Identity withheld. (personal communication, October 2022).

## HENNEPIN COUNTY
## MEDICAL EXAMINER'S OFFICE
## AUTOPSY REPORT

**ME NO.:** 20-3700

**CASE TITLE:** CARDIOPULMONARY ARREST COMPLICATING LAW ENFORCEMENT SUBDUAL, RESTRAINT, AND NECK COMPRESSION

**DECEASED:** George Floyd aka Floyd Perry    **SEX:** M    **AGE:** 46

**DATE AND HOUR OF DEATH:** 5-25-20; 9:25 p.m.

**DATE AND HOUR OF AUTOPSY:** 5-26-20; 9:25 a.m.

**PATHOLOGIST:** Andrew M. Baker, M.D.

**FINAL DIAGNOSES:**

46-year-old man who became unresponsive while being restrained by law enforcement officers; he received emergency medical care in the field and subsequently in the Hennepin HealthCare (HHC) Emergency Department, but could not be resuscitated.

I.  Blunt force injuries

     A.  Cutaneous blunt force injuries of the forehead, face, and upper lip

     B.  Mucosal injuries of the lips

     C.  Cutaneous blunt force injuries of the shoulders, hands, elbows, and legs

     D.  Patterned contusions (in some areas abraded) of the wrists, consistent with restraints (handcuffs)

II.  Natural diseases

     A.  Arteriosclerotic heart disease, multifocal, severe

     B.  Hypertensive heart disease

         1.  Cardiomegaly (540 g) with mild biventricular dilatation

         2.  Clinical history of hypertension

     C.  Left pelvic tumor (incidental, see microscopic description)

*Page 1 of George Floyd's autopsy report. The autopsy was conducted 12 hours after George Floyd died, but the report was not released until almost a week later. Baker, A. (2020, June 1). Cardiopulmonary arrest complicating law enforcement subdual, restraint, and neck compression. Hennepin County Medical Examiner's Office, ME NO 20-3700.*

George Floyd
20-3700
Page 2

III. No life-threatening injuries identified

    A.   No facial, oral mucosal, or conjunctival petechiae

    B.   No injuries of anterior muscles of neck or laryngeal structures

    C.   No scalp soft tissue, skull, or brain injuries

    D.   No chest wall soft tissue injuries, rib fractures (other than a single rib fracture from CPR), vertebral column injuries, or visceral injuries

    E.   Incision and subcutaneous dissection of posterior and lateral neck, shoulders, back, flanks, and buttocks negative for occult trauma

IV. Viral testing (Minnesota Department of Health, postmortem nasal swab collected 5/26/2020): positive for 2019-nCoV RNA by PCR (see 'Comments,' below)

V. Hemoglobin S quantitation (postmortem femoral blood, HHC Laboratory): 38% (see 'Comments,' below)

VI. Toxicology (see attached report for full details; testing performed on antemortem blood specimens collected 5/25/20 at 9:00 p.m. at HHC and on postmortem urine)

    A.   Blood drug and novel psychoactive substances screens:

        1.   Fentanyl 11 ng/mL

        2.   Norfentanyl 5.6 ng/mL

        3.   4-ANPP 0.65 ng/mL

        4.   Methamphetamine 19 ng/mL

        5.   11-Hydroxy Delta-9 THC 1.2 ng/mL; Delta-9 Carboxy THC 42 ng/mL; Delta-9 THC 2.9 ng/mL

        6.   Cotinine positive

        7.   Caffeine positive

    B.   Blood volatiles: negative for ethanol, methanol, isopropanol, or acetone

    C.   Urine drug screen: presumptive positive for cannabinoids, amphetamines, and fentanyl/metabolite

    D.   Urine drug screen confirmation: morphine (free) 86 ng/mL

*Page 2 of George Floyd's autopsy report.*

George Floyd
20-3700
Page 3

**Comments:** The finding of sickled-appearing cells in many of the autopsy tissue sections prompted the Hemoglobin S quantitation reported above.  This quantitative result is indicative of sickle cell trait.  Red blood cells in individuals with sickle cell trait are known to sickle as a postmortem artifact.  The decedent's antemortem peripheral blood smear (made from a complete blood count collected 5/25/20 at 9:00 p.m.) was reviewed by an expert HHC hematopathologist at the Medical Examiner's request.  This review found no evidence of antemortem sickling.

The decedent was known to be positive for 2019-nCoV RNA on 4/3/2020.  Since PCR positivity for 2019-nCoV RNA can persist for weeks after the onset and resolution of clinical disease, the autopsy result most likely reflects asymptomatic but persistent PCR positivity from previous infection.

6/1/2020

X  ~~Andrew M. Baker~~

Andrew M. Baker, M.D.
Chief Medical Examiner
Signed by: Andrew M. Baker MD
In accordance with HCME policy, this report was reviewed by another board-certified forensic pathologist prior to release.

*Page 3 of George Floyd's autopsy report.*

No mass lesions or areas of consolidation are present. The pulmonary vascular tree is free of thromboemboli. The tracheobronchial tree is free of blood, edema fluid, or foreign material.

**CARDIOVASCULAR SYSTEM:** The 540 g heart (upper limit of normal for body length is 510 g; upper limit of normal for body weight is 521 g)[1] is contained in an intact pericardial sac. The epicardial surface is smooth, with modest fat investment. The coronary arteries are present in a normal distribution, with a right dominant pattern. Cross sections of the vessels show multifocal atherosclerosis, with 75% proximal and 75% mid narrowing of the left anterior descending coronary artery; 75% proximal narrowing of the 1st diagonal branch of the left anterior descending coronary artery; 25% proximal narrowing of the circumflex coronary artery; and 90% proximal narrowing of the right coronary artery. The myocardium is homogeneous, red-brown, and firm. The valve leaflets are thin and mobile. The walls of the left and right ventricles are 1.2 and 0.4 cm thick, respectively. The endocardium is smooth and glistening. Both ventricular cavities are mildly dilated. The minimally atherosclerotic aorta gives rise to three intact and patent arch vessels. The renal and mesenteric vessels are unremarkable.

**LIVER AND BILIARY SYSTEM:** The 2565 g liver has an intact, smooth capsule and a sharp anterior border. The parenchyma is tan-brown and congested, with the usual lobular architecture. No mass lesions or other abnormalities are seen. The gallbladder contains a moderate amount of green-black bile and no stones. The mucosal surface is green and velvety. The extrahepatic biliary tree is patent.

**SPLEEN:** The 140 g spleen has a smooth, intact, red-purple capsule. The parenchyma is maroon and congested.

**PANCREAS:** The pancreas is firm and yellow-tan, with the usual lobular architecture. No mass lesions or other abnormalities are seen.

**ADRENALS:** The right and left adrenal glands are symmetric, with bright yellow cortices and gray medullae. No masses or areas of hemorrhage are identified.

---

[1] Kitzman DW, Scholz DG, Hagen PT, et al. Age-related changes in normal human hearts during the first 10 decades of life. Part II (maturity): a quantitative anatomic study of 765 specimens from subjects 20 to 99 years old. Mayo Clin Proc. 1988; 63: 137-146.

*Page 10 of George Floyd's autopsy report.*

**NMS Labs**
200 Welsh Road, Horsham, PA 19044-2208
Phone: (215) 657-4900 Fax: (215) 657-2972
e-mail: nms@nmslabs.com
Robert A. Middleberg, PhD, F-ABFT, DABCC-TC, Laboratory

CONFIDENTIAL

## Toxicology Report

**Report Issued**   05/31/2020 18:44

To:   **148889**
Hennepin County Medical Examiner
530 Chicago Avenue

Minneapolis, MN  55415

| | |
|---|---|
| **Patient Name** | FLOYD, GEORGE |
| **Patient ID** | 2020-3700 |
| **Chain** | NMSCP59310 |
| **Age** 46 Y | **DOB** 10/14/1973 |
| **Gender** | Male |
| **Workorder** | 20159963 |

Page 1 of 7

### Positive Findings:

| Compound | Result | Units | Matrix Source |
|---|---|---|---|
| Caffeine | Positive | mcg/mL | 001 - Hospital Blood |
| Cotinine | Positive | ng/mL | 001 - Hospital Blood |
| 4-ANPP | 0.65 | ng/mL | 003 - Hospital Blood |
| 11-Hydroxy Delta-9 THC | 1.2 | ng/mL | 001 - Hospital Blood |
| Delta-9 Carboxy THC | 42 | ng/mL | 001 - Hospital Blood |
| Delta-9 THC | 2.9 | ng/mL | 001 - Hospital Blood |
| Methamphetamine | 19 | ng/mL | 001 - Hospital Blood |
| Fentanyl | 11 | ng/mL | 001 - Hospital Blood |
| Norfentanyl | 5.6 | ng/mL | 001 - Hospital Blood |
| Cannabinoids | Presump Pos | ng/mL | 012 - Urine |
| Amphetamines | Presump Pos | ng/mL | 012 - Urine |
| Fentanyl / Metabolite | Presump Pos | ng/mL | 012 - Urine |
| Morphine - Free | 86 | ng/mL | 012 - Urine |

See Detailed Findings section for additional information

### Testing Requested:

| Analysis Code | Description |
|---|---|
| 8050U | Postmortem, Urine Screen Add-on (6-MAM Quantification only) |
| 9096B | Alcohol Screen, Blood (Forensic) |
| 8210B | Novel Psychoactive Substances (NPS) Screen 2, Blood |
| 8052B | Postmortem, Expanded, Blood (Forensic) |
| 8756B | Novel Psychoactive Substances (NPS) Screen 1, Blood |

### Specimens Received:

| ID | Tube/Container | Volume/ Mass | Collection Date/Time | Matrix Source | Miscellaneous Information |
|---|---|---|---|---|---|
| 001 | Lavender Vial | 2.8 mL | 05/25/2020 21:00 | Hospital Blood | |
| 002 | Gray Vial | 0.6 mL | 05/25/2020 21:00 | Hospital Blood | |
| 003 | Lavender Vial | 5.75 mL | 05/25/2020 21:00 | Hospital Blood | |
| 004 | Light Blue Vial | 2.5 mL | 05/25/2020 21:00 | Hospital Blood | |
| 005 | Green Vial | 1.3 mL | 05/25/2020 21:00 | Hospital Blood | |
| 006 | Red Vial | 0.75 mL | 05/25/2020 21:00 | Hospital Serum or Plasma | |
| 007 | Gray Top Tube | 8.8 mL | 05/26/2020 12:20 | Femoral Blood | |
| 008 | Gray Top Tube | 8.8 mL | 05/26/2020 12:20 | Femoral Blood | |
| 009 | Gray Top Tube | 8.8 mL | 05/26/2020 12:20 | Femoral Blood | |

NMS v.18.0

*Page 1 of George Floyd's toxicology report (page 14 in the overall autopsy report).*

## This Could Be Called an Overdose

The autopsy was conducted on May 26, 2020. But the official autopsy report was released about a week later on June 1st. In between, county attorneys met with Dr. Baker, the medical examiner who conducted the autopsy of George Floyd. Along with the obvious findings, the autopsy report—and the notes and memos from the county attorneys themselves—show how the facts were known, but quickly began to change. Even Dr. Baker himself appeared to change his opinion that week. Both Derek Chauvin and his defense attorney Eric Nelson, realized how Dr. Baker seemed to move away from his initial findings when he later testified during two federal grand jury hearings. He seemed to do the same thing during Derek Chauvin's trial in state court. Derek simply couldn't understand why Dr. Baker seemed to be changing his mind.

However, no matter how his testimony may have changed, or how the prosecution may have been lying by omission, the facts remain. During the meetings that took place the week after George Floyd died, county attorneys seemed well aware that heart diseases, drugs, and other factors played a role in his death. As written in their own notes, and even their own handwriting, prosecutors acknowledged several key findings:[62]

> "the ultimate cause of death may prove to be a multifactorial diagnosis"

> "the three factors in that diagnosis could be (1) coronary artery disease, (2) any stimulants potentially in Mr. Floyd's system causing the heart to work harder, and (3) the exertion caused by Mr. Floyd's encounter with the police officers"

> "The autopsy revealed no physical evidence that Mr. Floyd died from asphyxiation"

---

62. Exhibits submitted during the trial; State of Minnesota v. Derek Chauvin, 27-CR-20-12646.

"did not exhibit signs of petechiae, damage to his airways"

"Mr. Floyd had preexisting health conditions including [a] heavy heart and some coronary artery disease, including at least one artery that was approximately 75% blocked"

"No bruising on neck"

"No bruises on back or evidence of blunt trauma to back"

"most cases of untreated hypertension can put you at risk for death"

"get to death quicker because it [the heart] needs more oxygen and certain intoxicants can exacerbate"

"meth's bad for your heart"

"Baker did not watch videos before autopsy"

"From videos I have seen, it appears like his knee is on the side of his neck, not where the structures are"

"if found dead at home alone and no other apparent causes, this could be acceptable to call an O.D. [overdose]"

In other words, there was plenty of evidence for reasonable doubt—and plenty of reason to doubt that Floyd was "murdered."

27-CR-20-12646

# Exhibit 6

### WITNESS CONTACT FORM

**State of Minnesota v.**
**Derek Michael Chauvin, Tou Thao, J. Alexander Kueng, Thomas Kiernan Lane Hennepin**
**County Court File No.**
**27-CR-12646, 27-CR-20-12949, 27-CR-20-12953, 27-CR-20-12951**

Witness Name  Dr. Andrew Baker

Date          June 1, 2020

__X__  Witness statement(s) consistent with prior statement(s).

__X__  No new information provided.

__X__  Witness provided the following new information:

Met w/ Dr. Baker at ACO. Present were Matt Frank,
David Voigt, John Keller, Dionne Dodd, Beth Stark

Autopsy performed May 26 in a.m. Showed slides/photos
from autopsy. Abrasions on face consistent w/ being
on face + on left side. No petechiae in eyelids. No
bruising in neck on any muscles or injuries to structures
Bruise (R) shoulder, abrasion (L) shoulder. Wrists show
typical marks from handcuffs. Sternum is fractured + a
rib fracture - appears to be from medical device. No bruises
on back, or evidence of blunt trauma to back.
Baker did not watch videos before autopsy.
Heart is at upper limit of size, + w/ most cases. If untreated
hypertension p can put you at risk for death - get to
death quicker because it needs more oxygen And
certain intoxicants can exacerbate.
Specimens for lab testing were drawn at HCMC - This is
better than at autopsy, more accurately reflects actual at
death.

022935

27-CR-20-12646

Filed in Distric
State of Min
8/28/2020 4:

6/1/20 p. 2

Fentany at 11 ng/ml - this is higher than chronic pain patient. If he were found dead at home alone & no other apparent causes, this <u>could be acceptable to call an OD.</u> Deaths have been certified of level of 3.

Baker- I am not saying this killed him,

4fentanyl: metabolite

4AMP - think this is non-commercial

meth 19 ng/ml - this is relatively low, but meth is bad for your heart

<u>From videos I have seen,</u> it appears like his <u>knee is on the side of his neck</u>, not where the structures are

022936

*Exhibit—Motion to disqualify. State of Minnesota v. Derek Chauvin, 27-CR-20-12646 (August 28, 2020).*

27-CR-20-12646

Filed
Sta
8/2i

**HENNEPIN COUNTY ATTORNEY'S OFFICE**
**Community Prosecution Division**
**M E M O R A N D U M**

TO:     **State v. Derek Chauvin - file**

FROM:   **Amy Sweasy**

RE:     **Notes from conversation with Dr. Andrew Baker, Chief Hennepin County**
        **Medical Examiner**

DATE:   **June 1, 2020**

---

On May 31, 2020 at 7:30 p.m., Assistant Hennepin County Attorney Patrick Lofton and I met with Dr. Andrew Baker (AB) on Microsoft Teams. All three of us were in different locations. Dr. Baker said he had (and had recently received) the final toxicology results from Mr. George Floyd's samples which were analyzed by NMS labs.

AB shared his screen and showed us the results. He said that where it says, "Hospital Blood," those samples are from Mr. Floyd's hospital admission and were not acquired at autopsy. AB said that these samples are better for determining actual blood toxicity than samples taken at autopsy. Samples taken at autopsy may have undergone "post mortem distribution."

AB walked us down the list of substances for which NMS labs tested. Those values he highlighted were:

     4ANPP – a precursor and metabolite of fentanyl present in Mr. Floyd's blood.

     Methamphetamine – 19 ng/ML which he described as "very near the low end" and "a stimulant hard on the heart."

     Fentanyl – 11. He said, "that's pretty high." This level of fentanyl can cause pulmonary edema. Mr. Floyd's lungs were 2-3x their normal weight at autopsy. That is a fatal level of fentanyl under normal circumstances.

     Norfentanyl – 5.6 a metabolite of fentanyl.

Mr. Floyd's urine was tested for 4 things and are redundant, given the blood analysis. AB said, "the only thing that matters is what's in his blood."

AB said that if Mr. Floyd had been found dead in his home (or anywhere else) and there were no other contributing factors he would conclude that it was an overdose death.

*Exhibit — Motion to disqualify. State of Minnesota v. Derek Chauvin, 27-CR-20-12646*
*(August 28, 2020).*

27-CR-20-12646

Filed in [
State c
8/28/2(

---

**HENNEPIN COUNTY ATTORNEY'S OFFICE**
**Adult Prosecution Division**
**M E M O R A N D U M**

---

TO:     **File**

FROM:   **Patrick Lofton**

RE:     **George Floyd – UDF Case**
        **Meeting with Medical Examiner**

DATE:   **May 26, 2020**

---

On May 27, 2020, Patrick Lofton, Amy Sweasy, Mike Freeman, and Andrew LeFevour met with Hennepin County Medical Examiner Dr. Andrew Baker in person in a socially distanced room.

Dr. Baker provided the same autopsy presentation from the May 26, 2020 Microsoft Teams Meeting, as well as the following additional information:

Some of the scars on Mr. Floyd's hand were preexisting and likely from an incident in which he broke some glass and was admitted to the hospital approximately a month prior.

AB recalled there were indications in Mr. Floyd's medical records that he had been admitted to methamphetamine detox.

AB reiterated that his findings are preliminary and that he has not issued a final report. He opined the ultimate cause of death may prove to be a multifactorial diagnosis. Based on what AB knows so far, the three factors in that diagnosis could be (1) coronary artery disease, (2) any stimulants potentially in Mr. Floyd's system causing his heart to work harder, and (3) the exertion caused by Mr. Floyd's encounter with the police officers. This would depend on the quality and intensity of the encounter.

In AB's experience, overexertion of the heart is one of the reason police departments avoid using the type of hold at issue. AB still had not seen any videos.

*Exhibit—Motion to disqualify. State of Minnesota v. Derek Chauvin, 27-CR-20-12646 (August 28, 2020).*

## The "Commissioned" Autopsy Review

For some, the preliminary findings and the official autopsy report had to be refuted because it contradicted what they wanted to believe. Fortunately, there was an autopsy *review* provided by doctors "commissioned" by George Floyd's family. Their review perfectly fit the narrative and the accusations about how Floyd died, which seems questionable. The review was released basically at the same time as the official autopsy report, which also seemed a bit odd. The review diverted attention from the official autopsy report and forced a comparison with the "opinions" from the doctors hired by the family.

Unlike the official report, the review insisted that Floyd died from asphyxiation. They apparently refuted the fact that he died from cardiac arrest. Instead, they believed that "mechanical asphyxia" caused his death. As if that was telling enough, they also implied that no other conditions or factors contributed to his death. This resembles Mayor Frey's perspective. Frey didn't seem to care about what the investigation would reveal. Instead, he believed what he saw in the video. Crump seemed to be telling everyone to do the same thing—ignore the official autopsy report and just believe what you saw. Crump basically said as much:[63]

> "What those officers did, as we have seen on the video, is his cause of death, not some underlying, unknown health condition. [...] George Floyd was a healthy young man. [...] George died because he needed a breath ... He needed a breath of air."

Crump's statement defies common sense on so many levels. Although it's an attractive piece of persuasion. I mean, who wouldn't want to believe that you're healthy (so long as you are unaware of the diseases you have). But the

---

63. Donaghue, E. (2020, June 4). Two autopsies both find George Floyd died by homicide, but differ on some key details. *CBS News.*

suggestion that "what you don't know can't kill you" defies reality. Frankly, it's abhorrent and absurd. There's a reason why hypertension, which George Floyd had, is known as "the silent killer" and part of a global health crisis.[64]

## Ignoring the Facts

The claim that George Floyd was "healthy" not only defies reason, it ignores the diseases that he had that were listed in the autopsy report. Apparently, COVID, illegal drugs, and severe health problems—like heart disease and hypertension—had *nothing* to do with his death. Focusing on how he couldn't breathe brings up another odd coincidence. One of the doctors hired by the family, Dr. Baden, also conducted an autopsy of Eric Garner. Garner died from an asthma attack while being arrested by NYPD officers in 2014. Incidentally, his last words were "I can't breathe," which became a rallying cry for those protesting police brutality. Protesters also took up the "I can't breathe" mantra after the death of Floyd, since he said the same thing. It's difficult to ignore the connection, as though the deaths of Garner and Floyd were part of a "long history" of racist police brutality and Black men being choked by police officers.[65] But Floyd didn't die from a chokehold or an asthma attack.

The official autopsy report indicated that Floyd died from cardiac arrest—his heart and breathing suddenly stopped. The report also indicated other significant factors, including that he had methamphetamine in his system and a significant amount of fentanyl. Fentanyl is an opioid considered to be 80 to 200 times stronger than morphine.[66] Like other opioids, the effects of fentanyl include confusion, nausea, breathing problems, and unconsciousness. And one of the most common signs of an opioid overdose includes "slow, shallow,

---

64. A global brief on hypertension: silent killer, global public health crisis: World Health Day 2013 (No. WHO/DCO/WHD/2013.2). (2013). *World Health Organization*.
65. Tatter, G., & Chakrabarti, M. (2020, June 1). Death of George Floyd: A long history of racism in America. *WBUR*.
66. Fentanyl drug facts. (2021, June 1). *National Institute on Drug Abuse*.

irregular or no breathing."[67] Mixing fentanyl with other drugs increases the likelihood of a fatal interaction.[68] According to the National Institute on Drug Abuse (NIDA), "when people overdose on fentanyl, their breathing can slow or stop." Unfortunately, cardiac arrest caused by an opioid overdose has become a significant cause of death in the United States.[69] However, the independent autopsy review didn't mention any of this. Neither did Crump. Apparently, the media and the Left were trying to ignore these inconvenient facts. For example, an article in *The New York Times* glossed over all of this:[70]

> "The one-page summary also noted that Mr. Floyd was intoxicated with fentanyl and had recently used methamphetamines."

The suggestion that George Floyd "recently used methamphetamines" seems questionable. Again, the official report provided three undeniable facts:

> First, George Floyd had COVID, heart diseases, and a combination of drugs in his system.

> Second, he died because his heart suddenly stopped and so did his breathing due to cardiac arrest, or more specifically, "cardiopulmonary arrest."

> Third, there was no indication that Floyd was physically choked or strangled.

---

67. US Department of Health & Human Services, DHHS. (2019). Publication No. 2019–127.

68. Facts about fentanyl. (2021). *The United States Department of Justice, Drug Enforcement Administration (DEA).*

69. Dezfulian, C., Orkin, A. M., et al. (2021, April 20). Opioid-associated out-of-hospital cardiac Arrest: Distinctive clinical features and implications for health care and public responses: A scientific statement from the American Heart Association," *Circulation, 143*(16).

70 Robles, R., & Burch, A. (2020, June 2). How did George Floyd die? Here's what we know. *The New York Times.*

**An Autopsy Review — Based on A Viral Facebook Video**

Aside from the difference in findings, there was an enormous difference in procedure between the official autopsy report and the commissioned private "review." As noted in a memo written by Hennepin County Attorney Patrick Lofton:[71]

> "He [Dr. Baker] specifically avoided watching any videos associated with the case to avoid a bias during the autopsy."

In preparing the private autopsy review, the "independent" doctors hired by George Floyd's family, Dr. Wilson and Dr. Baden, clearly relied upon the viral cellphone video. Dr. Baden concluded that:

> "The cause of death is consistent with what we see in the video."

In following Dr. Baden's apparent merry-go-round logic, the manner of George Floyd's death was a "homicide as seen in the video" because "the cause of death is consistent with what we see in the video." This hardly proves anything — except that Dr. Baden did not avoid video bias. Likewise, Dr. Wilson echoed the opinion of Dr. Baden. Although, Dr. Wilson skipped the circular reasoning and offered more scientific-sounding findings. Nonetheless, they were still based on the Facebook video. Their opinions might sound fancy, but they do not explain why George Floyd said "I can't breathe" before Derek Chauvin even touched him. But then again, that wasn't in the viral Facebook video, either.

---

71. Exhibit A. Memo regarding the procedure followed by Hennepin County Medical Examiner Dr. Andrew Baker to avoid bias. Motion to disqualify. State of Minneapolis v. Derek Chauvin, 27-CR-20-12646 (August 28, 2020).

Adding to the confusion, few news stations and media outlets pointed out the significant difference between the official autopsy report and the *review* commissioned by Floyd's family. But only one was based on an actual autopsy examination. Even the news station where I worked, *WCCO*, put out misleading headlines such as: "2 Autopsies Released in George Floyd's Death, From Hennepin County and Independent Group."[72] Even the fact that the word *independent* made it into that headline is an example of media manipulation. There's nothing independent about two medical professionals on the family's dime being paid to offer their opinions.

---

72. 2 Autopsies released in George Floyd's death, from Hennepin County and independent group. (2020, June 1). WCCO, *CBS Minnesota.*

27-CR-20-12646

## Subject: Medical Examiners' Findings.

Good afternoon,

The Floyd family has enlisted the assistance of the following Independent Medical Examiners:

1. Dr. Michael Baden
2. Dr. Allecia Wilson

Dr. Baden and Dr. Wilson have been unable to complete their final reports as we are still awaiting Data Practices Act (FOIA) responses and requests for the microscopic slides, pictures, and other evidence gathered during Dr. Baker's initial autopsy of Mr. Floyd. We have requested all of these materials but have yet to receive them.

From their autopsies Dr. Baden and Dr. Wilson came to the following findings that were summarized at the June 1, 2020 press conference:

1. Dr. Baden
   a. Cause of Death: Mr. Floyd died of traumatic asphyxia due to the compression of his neck and back during restraint by police.
   b. Manner of Death: Homicide as seen in the scene video and confirmed at autopsy.
   c. The pressure on the neck interfered with blood flow to his brain and air flow to and from his lungs. The pressure on his back while in the prone position prevented his diaphragm from moving so he couldn't inhale.
   d. The cause of death is consistent with what we see on the video.

2. Dr. Wilson
   a. Cause of Death: Asphyxia due to neck and back compression led to a lack of blood flow to the brain.
   b. Mechanical asphyxia defined as a physical force that interferes with breathing or the delivery of oxygen to the organs. In this case, the physical force was neck and chest compression.
   c. Based on the video and the position of the knee in the video, there was pressure on the carotid artery of the neck that led to cerebral

*Memo regarding the opinions of the autopsy review. Motion to Disqualify. State of Minnesota v. Derek Chauvin, 27-CR-20-12646 (August 28, 2020).*

**HENNEPIN COUNTY ATTORNEY'S OFFICE**
**Adult Prosecution Division**
**M E M O R A N D U M**

**TO:**     **File**

**FROM:**   **Patrick Lofton**

**RE:**     **George Floyd – UDF Case**
          **Meeting with Medical Examiner**

**DATE:**   **May 26, 2020**

---

On May 26, 2020, Patrick Lofton and Amy Sweasy met with Hennepin County Medical Examiner Dr. Andrew Baker (AB) over Microsoft Teams. Also present in the MS Teams meeting were SAIC Scott Mueller and SA Mike Phill from the BCA and FBI Agents Hoffstetter, Rainer, Kane, and Melcher.

AB explained his findings from the autopsy of George Floyd. He stated that his final report is not complete and that he must review more evidence, including video evidence, and toxicology results before releasing a final opinion.

The autopsy revealed no physical evidence suggesting that Mr. Floyd died of asphyxiation. Mr. Floyd did not exhibit signs of petechiae, damage to his airways or thyroid, brain bleeding, bone injuries, or internal bruising.

Mr. Floyd had several external injuries, including a laceration to his lip and bruising on his left shoulder and face. He also had abrasions on his fingers and knuckles as well as wrist injuries likely associated with being handcuffed.

Mr. Floyd had preexisting health conditions including a heavy heart and some coronary artery disease, including at least one artery that was approximately 75% blocked.

AB sent Mr. Floyd's blood samples to NMS Labs, who will provide a full toxicology report.

AB opined that he does not have a full context for Mr. Floyd's death without reviewing more of the evidence. He specifically avoided watching any videos associated with the case to avoid a bias during the autopsy.

*Memo regarding the autopsy by Hennepin County Medical Examiner Dr. Andrew Baker. Motion to disqualify. State of Minnesota v. Derek Chauvin, 27-CR-20-12646 (August 28, 2020).*

## The Other Autopsy Review

As if things weren't complicated enough, the DOJ needed its own "independent" review. The DOJ requested The Office of the Armed Forces Medical Examiner to conduct their own review of Dr. Baker's autopsy findings and offer their own opinion. This review was completed on June 10, 2020 and referenced both the official Hennepin County autopsy report and the private autopsy review requested by George Floyd's family. In offering an opinion to the DOJ, the Armed Forces Medical Examiner concluded:

> "The Office of the Armed Forces Medical Examiner agrees with the autopsy findings and the cause of death certification of George Floyd as determined by the Hennepin County Medical Examiner's Office."

In their opinion—based on group consensus—"all" of the staff that took part in this "review conference" agreed that George Floyd's death was a homicide. They listed *three* contributing factors:

> "His death was caused by <u>police subdual and restraint</u> in the setting of <u>severe hypertensive atherosclerotic cardiovascular disease</u>, and <u>methamphetamine and fentanyl intoxication</u>."

In other words, George Floyd's death was apparently caused by illegal drugs, heart disease, and the fact that he was resisting arrest and had to be restrained. This contradicted the autopsy review by the doctors hired by the family and their opinions which Crump wanted everyone to believe. This also contradicted the blind-eye insistence that nothing but "systemic police racism" killed him. The copy that was submitted to the court is basically illegible and has been reproduced here to make it easier to read.

**Armed Forces Medical**
**Examiner System**

**DEFENSE HEALTH AGENCY**
**115 PURPLE HEART DRIVE**
**DOVER AIR FORCE BASE, DELAWARE 19902**

**CASE CONSULT**

**DATE: 10 June 2020**                    **ACCESSION NUMBER: C0022-20**
                                          **NAME: George Perry Floyd**

**ME CASE NUMBER: ME20-3700 (Hennepin County Medical Examiner's Office)**

**CONTRIBUTOR:** US Department of Justice

**CAUSE OF DEATH:** Cardiopulmonary arrest complicating law enforcement subdual, restraint, and neck compression

**MANNER OF DEATH:** Homicide

**MATERIALS REVIEWED:** Case file including autopsy photographs; Minnesota Police Department General Offense Hardcopy (incident date 5/25/2020); Hennepin County Autopsy report (Dr. Andrew Baker); Video footage from police body cameras and surveillance cameras; emergency medical services and emergency department medical records; interview documents from Federal Bureau of Investigations.

**SYNOPSIS:**

George Perry Floyd was a 46 year old African-American male who died while in police custody on 25 May 2020 in Minneapolis, MN. Per report, Mr. Floyd was detained under suspicion of forgery. Upon review of the police body camera footage, he was handcuffed and became extremely agitated when officers attempted to place him into a police vehicle. In the subsequent struggle, he was taken to the ground in the prone position with his hands cuffed behind his back, one officer placing a knee on the back of Mr. Floyd's neck, and a second officer placing a knee on his buttocks/upper thigh region. While he was held in this position for over 9 minutes, Mr. Floyd gradually became devoid of purposeful speech and motion before becoming unresponsive. Upon arrival by emergency medical services, resuscitation efforts were initiated and were ultimately unsuccessful.

The initial autopsy was performed by Dr. Andrew Baker, Chief Medical Examiner of the Hennepin County Medical Examiner's Office. Significant findings included, but were not limited to, multiple abrasions and contusions consistent with the subdual and restraint, and hypertensive atherosclerotic cardiovascular disease with severe coronary artery atherosclerosis. Of note, no petechial hemorrhages were identified in the conjunctivae and oral mucosa, the layered neck

FOR OFFICIAL USE ONLY and may be exempt from mandatory disclosure under FOIA. DoD 5400.7R, "DoD Freedom of Information Act Program", DoD Directive 5230.9, "Clearance of DoD Information for Public Release", and DoD Instruction 5230.29, "Sensitivity and Policy Review of DoD Information for Public Release" apply.

*While the quality of the original is poor, it evidences the early involvement of the federal government in this case. Page 1 of 2, Exhibit 19. Consult Report C0022-20 from the Director of the Office of the Armed Forces Medical Examiner, Motion to dismiss. State of Minnesota v. Derek Chauvin, 27-CR-20-12646 (August 28, 2020).*

CONSULT REPORT: C0022-20
Floyd, George Perry

Page 2 of 2

dissection and the posterior neck were absent of hemorrhage, and there were no fractures of the hyoid bone or thyroid cartilage. Toxicologic examination was positive for methamphetamine, fentanyl, and metabolites of tetrahydrocannabinol (THC) in hospital blood samples. Swab testing for COVID-19 was positive, however there were no gross or histologic findings consistent with an active COVID-19 infection. Mr. Floyd was noted to have a previously positive COVID-19 test on 4/3/2020. Ancillary testing was positive for sickle cell trait and examination of an antemortem peripheral blood smear (drawn 5/25/20 at 2100) demonstrated no evidence of antemortem sickling.

The United States Department of Justice requested an independent evaluation of the Hennepin County Autopsy Report and its conclusions by the Office of the Armed Forces Medical Examiner. A private second autopsy was performed by Dr. Michael Baden at request of the family. Dr. Baden's report is unavailable at the time of this consultation.

OPINION:

The Office of the Armed Forces Medical Examiner agrees with the autopsy findings and the cause of death certification of George Floyd as determined by the Hennepin County Medical Examiner's Office. His death was caused by the police subdual and restraint in the setting of severe hypertensive atherosclerotic cardiovascular disease, and methamphetamine and fentanyl intoxication. The subdual and restraint had elements of positional and mechanical asphyxiation. The presence of sickle cell trait is a significant finding in this context.

We concur with the reported manner of death of homicide.

This case was reviewed in a staff consultation review conference. All are in concurrence with the synopsis and opinion of this report.

URIBE.PAUL.S Digitally signed by
HANE.117608 URIBE.PAUL.SHANE.11
7826 Date:2020.06.10
13:47:36 -04'00'
_____
Paul S. Uribe M.D.
LTC MC USA
Director, Office of the Armed Forces Medical Examiner

FINELLI.LOUIS.N Digitally signed by
FINELLI.LOUIS.NIEL.1020287418
IEL.1020287418 Date:2020.06.10 18:22:00
-04'00'
_____
Louis N. Finelli D.O.
COL MC USA
Armed Forces Medical Examiner

*Page 2 of 2, Exhibit 19. Consult Report C0022-20 from the Director of the Office of the Armed Forces Medical Examiner, Motion to dismiss. State of Minnesota v. Derek Chauvin, 27-CR-20-12646 (August 28, 2020).*

**DEFENSE HEALTH AGENCY**
115 PURPLE HEART DRIVE
DOVER AIR FORCE BASE, DELAWARE 19902

**CASE CONSULT**

**DATE: 10 June 2020**                              **ACCESSION NUMBER; C0022-20**
                                                        **NAME: George Perry Floyd**

**ME CASE NUMBER; ME20-3700 (Hennepin County Medical Examiner's Office)**

**CONTRIBUTOR: US Department of Justice**

**CAUSE OF DEATH: Cardiopulmonary arrest complicating law enforcement subdual, restraint, and neck compression**

**MANNER OF DEATH: Homicide**

**MATERIALS REVIEWED: Case file including <u>autopsy photographs; Minnesota</u> Police Department General Offense Hardcopy (incident date <u>5/25/2020); Hennepin County</u> Autopsy report (Dr. Andrew Baker); Video footage from police body cameras and surveillance cameras; emergency medical services and emergency department medical <u>records; interview documents from Federal Bureau of Investigation.</u>**

**SYNOPSIS:**
  George Perry Floyd was a 46 year old African-American male who died while in police custody on <u>25 May 2020</u> in Minneapolis, MN. Per report, Mr. Floyd was detained under <u>suspicion of forgery</u>. Upon review of the police body camera footage, he was <u>handcuffed and</u> became extremely agitated when officers <u>attempted</u> to place him into a police vehicle. In the subsequent struggle, he was taken to the ground in the prone position with his hands cuffed behind his back, one officer placing a knee on the back of Mr. Floyd's neck, and a second officer placing a knee on his buttocks/upper thigh region. While he was held in this position for over 9 <u>minutes,</u> Mr. Floyd gradually became devoid <u>of purposeful</u> speech and motion before <u>becoming</u> unresponsive. Upon arrival by <u>emergency</u> medical services, resuscitation efforts were initiated and were ultimately unsuccessful.
  The initial autopsy was <u>performed</u> by Dr. Andrew Baker, Chief Medical Examiner of the Hennepin County Medical <u>Examiner's</u> Office. Significant findings included, but were not limited to, multiple <u>abrasions</u> and contusions <u>consistent</u> with the subdual and restraint, and hypertensive arteriosclerotic <u>cardiovascular disease</u> with severe <u>coronary artery</u> atherosclerosis. Of note, no petechial hemorrhages were identified in the <u>conjunctivae</u> and oral mucosa, the layered neck

*Reproduction of page 1 of 2, Exhibit 19. Consult Report C0022-20 from the Director of the Office of the Armed Forces Medical Examiner, Motion to dismiss. State of Minnesota v. Derek Chauvin, 27-CR-20-12646 (August 28, 2020); document reproduced by Dr. JC Chaix.*

dissection and the posterior neck were absent of hemorrhage, and there were no fractures of the hyoid bone or thyroid cartilage. Toxicologic examination was positive for methamphetamine, fentanyl, and metabolites of tetrahydrocannabinol (THC) in hospital blood samples. Swab testing for COVID-19 was positive, however there were no gross or histologic findings consistent with an active COVID-19 infection. Mr. Floyd was noted to have a previously positive COVID-19 test on 4/3/2020. Ancillary testing was positive for sickle cell trait and examination of an antemortem peripheral blood smear (drawn 5/25/20 at 2100) demonstrated no evidence of antemortem sickling.

The United States Department of Justice requested an independent evaluation of the Hennepin County Autopsy Report and its conclusions by the Office of the Armed Forces Medical Examiner. A private second autopsy was performed by Dr. Michael Baden at request of the family. Dr. Baden's report is unavailable at the time of this consultation.

**OPINION:**

The Office of the Armed Forces Medical Examiner agrees with the autopsy findings and the cause of death certification of George Floyd as determined by the Hennepin County Medical Examiner's Office. His death was caused by police subdual and restraint in the setting of severe hypertensive atherosclerotic cardiovascular disease, and methamphetamine and fentanyl intoxication. The subdual and restraint had elements of positional and mechanical asphyxiation. The presence of sickle cell trait is a significant finding in this context.

We concur with the reported manner of death of homicide.

This case was reviewed in a staff consultation review conference. All are in concurrence with the synopsis and opinion of this report.

{Digital signature}

_____
Paul S. Uribe M.D.
LTC MC USA
Director, Office of the Armed Forces Medical Examiner

{Digital signature}

_____
Louis N. Finell D.O.
COL MC USA
Armed Forces Medical Examiner

*Reproduction of page 2 of 2, Exhibit 19. Consult Report C0022-20 from the Director of the Office of the Armed Forces Medical Examiner, Motion to dismiss. State of Minnesota v. Derek Chauvin, 27-CR-20-12646 (August 28, 2020).*

## What the Viral Video Doesn't Show

Obviously, there was nothing straightforward about any of this considering there was an official autopsy report, an autopsy review paid for by the family, and another review by the Office of the Armed Forces Medical Examiner. But they all share something in common—most of the critical findings can't be seen in the viral video. Granted, the video of Officer Derek Chauvin kneeling on George Floyd looks bad. However, looks can be deceiving. For example, the official autopsy report clearly indicated that Floyd had "No life-threatening injuries identified." In other words, Floyd didn't die from having his neck crushed "into the pavement" as the ACLU and many others insisted.[73] This fact alone contradicts what the media and the Left were forcing the rest of us to believe.

### George Floyd Had Heart Diseases

As listed in the official autopsy report—and referenced in the review by the Office of the Armed Forces Medical Examiner—Floyd had three diseases. He had a "left pelvic tumor," but it wasn't life-threatening. Although Floyd had two other diseases that posed significant health concerns. The first was "arteriosclerotic heart disease." The other was "hypertensive heart disease," which is related to high blood pressure and hypertension—aka the "silent killer." Shortness of breath and difficulty breathing are common symptoms of both diseases along with higher risks for COVID-19 complications. Both diseases also cause heart attacks and strokes.[74] But there's no way anyone could have known any of this from watching a video on Facebook.

---

73. ACLU responds to Minneapolis Police killing George Floyd. (May 26, 2020). *American Civil Liberties Union, ACLU of Minnesota.*

74. Andreadis, E. A. (2016). *Hypertension and cardiovascular disease.* Springer.

## George Floyd Had COVID When He Died

Most people didn't know that George Floyd had COVID-19 when he died. However, the official autopsy report indicated:

> "The decedent was known to be positive for 2019-nCoV RNA on 4/3/2020. Since PCR positivity for 2019-nCoV RNA can persist for weeks after the onset and resolution of clinical disease, the autopsy result most likely reflects asymptomatic but persistent PCR positivity from previous infection."

Notice there's nothing conclusive about Floyd's COVID-related symptoms, just what "most likely" was the case. But he clearly tested positive for COVID-19 on April 3, 2020—and still tested positive when the autopsy was conducted on May 26, 2020. The COVID pandemic was still in the early stages, but heart diseases were already known to cause severe, if not fatal COVID-related complications. The autopsy report also indicated that Floyd had "cotinine" in his system, which forms when nicotine from tobacco smoke enters the body.[75] Just as a reminder, this incident started because George Floyd went into a store to buy cigarettes with counterfeit money.[76] Along with heart disease, the Center for Disease Control (CDC) also listed smoking as a higher risk for severe COVID complications.

## George Floyd Had Fentanyl in His System

The autopsy report also indicated that George Floyd had several "compounds" in his system. These included caffeine and cotinine, along with THC (the active substance in marijuana), methamphetamine, norfentanyl, fentanyl, and

---

75. Benowitz, N. L. (1996). Cotinine as a biomarker of environmental tobacco smoke exposure. *Epidemiologic reviews*, 18(2), 188-204.
76. Pross, K. (2021, March 31). 19-year-old who sold George Floyd cigarettes before his arrest testifies in Derek Chauvin trial. *Pioneer Press*.

morphine. The autopsy also indicated how fentanyl can cause breathing problems and death:

> "Signs associated with fentanyl toxicity include severe respiratory depression, seizures, hypotension, coma and death. In fatalities from fentanyl, blood concentrations are variable and have been reported as low as 3 ng/mL."

The autopsy report indicated that George Floyd had 11 ng/mL of fentanyl in his system. That's nearly three times more than 3 ng/mL, an amount that has proven to be fatal. This could have complicated his ability to breathe, if not stopped his breathing altogether. Incidentally, the CDC listed drug abuse as another underlying factor of higher risk for severe COVID-19 complications. The autopsy review conducted by the Office of the Armed Forces Medical Examiner listed the combination of fentanyl and methamphetamine as a factor in George Floyd's death. With all that in mind, the autopsy report indicated that Floyd had three underlying conditions that pose higher risks for severe COVID complications according to the CDC: 1) heart diseases; 2) smoking; 3) drug abuse. Again, none of these could be seen in the Facebook video.

### Intent—According to Derek Chauvin in His Own Words...

Intent is also something that the autopsy report and the reviews do not cover. As the Hennepin County Medical Examiner's office noted, the cause of George Floyd's death "is not a legal determination of culpability or intent."[77] So, even though the autopsy "revealed no physical findings that support a diagnosis of traumatic asphyxia or strangulation," one could argue that the intent of Officer Derek Chauvin remains debatable. Unless you ask him yourself. As Derek explained:[78]

---

77. Donaghue, E. (2020, June 4). Two autopsies both find George Floyd died by homicide, but differ on some key details. *CBS News*.

78. D. Chauvin (personal communication, July 15, 2022).

"We weren't trying to murder anyone. He [Floyd] was resisting then something happened to him. So, we took him out of the car, and we were using MRT and waiting for EMS, like it says in policy."

The Maximal Restraint Technique, or MRT was approved by the Minneapolis Police Department.[79] It's not something officers use every day. But given the nature of police work, and combative suspects or people who are resisting arrest, it's a way for officers to safely subdue a subject—particularly ones who are having a violent drug-induced episode, experiencing excited delirium and likely to suffer cardiac arrest. That said, if seeing is believing—as Mayor Frey, Ben Crump, and others have insisted—then it's worth looking at MRT training materials.

One of the photos from MPD training looks remarkably similar to what Chauvin, Lane, Kueng, and Thao were doing when George Floyd was resisting arrest. Notice how the officer on the left *appears* to be "kneeling on the neck" of the officer on the ground. So even if you don't believe a word Derek Chauvin says, the MRT training materials and the lack of physical injuries to George Floyd's neck tell a completely different story than the narrative the media and the Left were promoting. Comparing the photo from MRT training and a screenshot from the Facebook video might offer a bit more insight.

---

79. Section 5-316, Maximal Restraint Technique, introduced and revised on May 29, 2002; June 13 2014; July 31, 2017; and April 2, 2018.

*Training materials from the Minneapolis Police Department. Exhibit 19, Motion to dismiss. State of Minnesota v. Derek Chauvin, 27-CR-20-12646 (August 28, 2020).*

*A photo from Minneapolis Police Department training materials (left) and a screenshot from bystander video of the arrest of George Floyd (right) showing the Maximal Restraint Technique (MRT); see Minneapolis Police Department Policy 5-316.*

If nothing else, the comparison shows Officer Chauvin and the other officers following MRT training procedures—not *intentionally* murdering someone in the street in front of a crowd of bystanders. MRT was part of Minneapolis Police training for years, even though Chief Arradondo, Mayor Frey, and so many others claimed it never was. As though they were trying to avoid the MRT, they kept talking about "neck restraints" and "chokeholds" or whatever else people believed they saw. Whenever there is a critical incident or an in-custody death, policy and training manuals are almost immediately reviewed. In this case, the policy and procedure manual mysteriously disappeared from the MPD website. About three weeks later, the use of force policy was revised on June 16, 2020 and available again.[80] The whole thing seemed awful strange, to say the least.

### Fentanyl & Wooden Chest Syndrome

Along with the findings of the official autopsy, there's something else that could have contributed to Floyd's death. It's called Wooden Chest Syndrome.[81] Fentanyl and other opioids can cause chest and neck muscles to stiffen like a wooden board and cause people to stop breathing. Healthcare professionals are aware that high doses of fentanyl can cause it, however drug users on the street may not be as aware.[82] Wooden Chest Syndrome first appeared in medical journals in 1953.[83] Since then, several studies have discussed the connections between fentanyl and respiratory failure. One study explained

---

80. Neck hold used by Minneapolis officer was approved by department policy. (2020, May 29). *Law Officer.*

81. Karch, S. B., & Drummer, O. (2015). *Karch's pathology of drug abuse* (fifth edition). Taylor & Francis.

82. Nath, J. (2021). *Sins against science: How misinformation affects our lives and laws.* McFarland.

83. Hamilton, W. K, & Cullen, S. C. (1953). Effect of levallorphan tartrate upon opiate induced respiratory depression, *Anesthesiology, 14,* 550-554.

how it also complicates COVID-19 and has led to fatalities.[84] Another explained how a 52-year-old man injected himself with fentanyl and other opioids at a drug treatment facility. Shortly afterward, the nursing staff found him sitting upright, but completely stiff, unresponsive, and not breathing—and obviously suffering from fentanyl-induced Wooden Chest Syndrome.[85] This could have been an isolated incident. Although another study found that among 500 patients who had a dose of fentanyl, 499 had some degree of muscle rigidity after "approximately 60–90 seconds," which makes Wooden Chest Syndrome seem more like a certainty than a probability. It also found that the muscle rigidity lasted "for about eight to 15 minutes."

Wooden Chest Syndrome can be fatal in minutes.[86] This could explain why George Floyd repeatedly said, "I can't breathe" *before* he was taken out of the police car and put on the ground. This could also explain why Floyd said, "My stomach hurts. My neck hurts. Everything hurts" while his right arm appeared to be stiffening.[87] But the strangest thing about Wooden Chest syndrome is that nobody seemed to be talking about it. When the autopsy report was released, *CNN*, *The New York Times*, *NPR*, *USA Today* and so many other media outlets didn't seem to ask many questions about the drugs in Floyd's system.[88]

---

84. Judd, G., Starcher, R., & Hotchkin, D. (2021, May 19). *Fentanyl-induced Wooden Chest Syndrome masquerading as severe respiratory distress syndrome in COVID-19.* Providence Portland Medical Center Internal Medicine.

85. Buxton, J. A., Gauthier, T., et al. (2018). A 52-year-old man with fentanyl-induced muscle rigidity. *CMAJ, 190*(17), E539-E541.

86. Kost, M. (2019). Moderate procedural sedation and analgesia: A question and answer approach, *Elsevier Health Sciences*, p. 93.

87. Transcript of Officer J. Alexander Kueng, Filed in District Court, State of Minnesota, 27-CR-20-12951, (July 7, 2020), p. 22.

88. Adone, D. (2021, April 9). Heart disease, fentanyl contributed to George Floyd's death but were not main cause, medical examiner says. *CNN*; Bogel-Burroughs, N. (2021, April 8). George Floyd showed signs of a brain injury 4 minutes before Derek Chauvin lifted his knee, a doctor testifies," *The New York Times*; Chappell, B., & Romo, V. (2021, April 8). Chauvin trial: Expert says George Floyd died from a lack of oxygen, not fentanyl. *NPR*; Sadeghi, M. (2021, April 21). Fact check: George Floyd's death ruled a homicide, Not fentanyl overdose. *USA Today*.

Instead, they attacked the idea that Floyd could have died from a fentanyl overdose, or anybody who even suggested the idea. It seemed like they were pushing a narrative and lying by omission. This isn't just media criticism. I witnessed this first-hand. I had been covering stories about opioid overdoses at *WCCO* for years, from the tragic deaths of high school students to the overdose of Prince, the popstar and Minnesota native. So, when I read the autopsy report, I remembered how people who overdosed on fentanyl and other opioids stopped breathing. After a few minutes of searching around, I found several recent articles in medical journals that mentioned Wooden Chest Syndrome. Again, I'm a news reporter, not a doctor. But there seemed to be some possible connection—especially since Wooden Chest Syndrome fit the findings of *both* the official autopsy report and the review on behalf of the family (and the other review requested by the DOJ).

## When the Media Stops Asking Questions, It's A Sign

It seemed odd that Wooden Chest Syndrome wasn't being mentioned on the news or social media. Maybe it had nothing to do with George Floyd's death, or maybe it explained everything, who knows. But Wooden Chest Syndrome seemed like something the media should've at least been questioning. I had been sharing things about police procedures and other details with the *WCCO* newsroom for years. Since I went through a citizen's police academy, which is something every crime reporter should do, I was often the go-to person for crime-related stories. Although with the George Floyd incident, most of what I was sharing was being ignored or dismissed. So, I didn't expect what I discovered about Wooden Chest Syndrome to get much attention or become a news story. Besides, *WCCO* seemed far more interested in sticking to the narrative than reporting facts. That's basically what happened in this case; I mentioned plenty of research about fentanyl, COVID, and Wooden Chest Syndrome and it was simply ignored. I remember thinking that if this kind of dismissiveness was going on in my own newsroom, it was certainly going on at other stations, where challenging the narrative was a career-ending move.

### Ignoring Facts & Telling Lies

Accepting the original findings of the autopsy would have destroyed the reputation of the left-wing media and it would have been a political nightmare. Everyone from Chief Arradondo to Mayor Frey, to Governor Walz to Senator Klobuchar, and even presidential candidate Joe Biden would have to admit they were wrong. Even worse, it would have only drawn more attention to their backward, "*guilty*-until-proven-innocent" rhetoric. Mob rule was everywhere. However, Biden offered up a picture-perfect example of how completely backward politicians were at the time. Before the autopsy was even started, Biden tweeted:[89]

> "George Floyd deserved better and his family deserves justice. His life mattered.
>
> I'm grateful for the swift action in Minneapolis to fire the officers involved—they must be held responsible for their egregious actions. The FBI should conduct a thorough investigation."

It's hard to ignore how Biden dismissed due process and publicly condemned the four officers. Since Biden was already "grateful" that the officers were fired for their "egregious actions," an investigation didn't seem necessary. Just like Mayor Frey, who believed what he saw and hardly cared about "whatever the investigation reveals," it seems Biden already declared that the officers were guilty until proven innocent. Obviously, he didn't have any of the facts because the investigation was still something the FBI *should* do. Speaking of

---

89. Joe Biden [@JoeBiden]. (2020, May 27). *George Floyd deserved better and his family deserves justice. His life mattered [...]* [Tweet] Twitter. https://twitter.com/JoeBiden/status/1265455605076185089

what should have been done in the name of justice, the findings of the autopsy report posed serious doubts about filing charges and prosecuting Derek Chauvin. The Hennepin County attorney's office basically admitted as much. The autopsy report, along with Officer Derek Chauvin's intentions, the MRT training provided by the Minneapolis Police Department, and the possibility of Wooden Chest Syndrome should have posed plenty of reasonable doubt and plenty of questions. But our so-called leaders already seemed to have all the answers about the "murder" of George Floyd.

# PART IV

## THE PROTESTS HIT HOME

## Bob Takes the Blame

A lot of people I've spoken with thought the autopsy report made the calls for "justice" seem like an *injustice*. It made the demands for arresting Derek Chauvin and the other officers seem like a witch hunt—especially since George Floyd didn't have *any* life-threatening injuries. They also said it made the media and the Left look bad, since none of their accusations seemed true. Consequently, more than a few politicians needed an excuse to cover up their mistakes. It wasn't like they were going to start apologizing to everyone. Besides, there was no looking back, the damage had already been done. So instead of telling the truth, they quickly began peddling "systemic police racism" and "racial inequalities" along with other "root causes" to justify the rampage and the riots in Minneapolis. But they also needed a scapegoat, someone they could make look even worse than them. That someone was Bob.

Yes, my husband, Bob Kroll, was to blame for the riots and "racism" in Minneapolis. This isn't an exaggeration. It was apparently "the truth" according to the media, the Left, and everybody else who followed along. Of course, plenty of Twitter trolls were pointing the finger at Bob. However, left-leaning politicians and even big-name organizations like the ACLU of Minnesota were also blaming Bob: [90]

> "Bob Kroll is the chief enabler of the racist, violent culture of policing in Minneapolis."

Bob thought it was odd that civil rights attorneys like Frey, Ellison, and those working for the ACLU were scapegoating him. They were accusing him of being a racist for speaking out on behalf of a mixed-race group of officers and the rest of the union members. He'd often ask, "How does supporting our officers—Whites, Blacks, Asians, all of them—make me or the union racist?"

---

90. ACLU of Minnesota [@ACLUMN]. (2020, June 23). *No Gale King interview can change [...]* [Tweet] Twitter. https://twitter.com/ACLUMN/status/1275447192266829824

He also thinks it's odd that the media and the Left still avoid answering that question. I, on the other hand, had a bit more insight about what was going on.

## Wokeness Hits the Newsroom

The news and media are supposed to scrutinize accusations, not automatically give them a platform. But when the riots started, anyone who challenged their narrative and woke agenda became a target. They were letting outrageous claims go unchecked out of fear of being called "racists" or not being "woke" enough. Bob was often critical of the media, so when he became a scapegoat, attacking him seemed to be a "justifiable" and even worthy cause. Doing so also fit the scheme of woke-minded mandates, at least the ones at WCCO, where I worked. We were even given a quota: half of the people interviewed for a story needed to be "people of color or from a protected class."[91] This wasn't fighting racism; this was putting it into practice. This forced reporters to judge people by *what* they were and the color of their skin—and compromised journalistic integrity and ethics. Along with the quotas, WCCO also established a new "anti-cop" mandate, like some other stations seemed to be doing. We were told to "attribute" information from the police and then provide "counter-narratives." In other words, we had to report what the police said, but then we had to report the opposite preferably spoken by someone who fit a quota. This wasn't news and perspective; this was media manipulation.

## Playing the "Opposite Game"

Ignoring reality and promoting the opposite seemed to be a political strategy the media and the Left were dogmatically following. Whatever the police had to say, they would strive to say the opposite. For example, Bob showed support for the four officers—two White officers, a Black officer, and an Asian officer along with the rest of the MPD—but he was labeled a "racist." He issued a statement asking people to remain calm and not rush to judgment, but

---

91. Identity withheld (personal communication, June 25, 2020).

the Minnesota ACLU called him an "enabler" of violence. Beyond name-calling, the more significant problem was that the media and the Left were manufacturing "counter-narratives" that hardly resembled reality. Meanwhile, protesters were attacking cops, trying to burn down police precincts, and demonstrating outside the police union. Since Bob was the reason for racism and the riots according to the ACLU, the media, and the Left, they were demanding "justice" —along with his resignation. Who knows how many hateful messages he was getting every hour along with hundreds of calls from reporters. Apparently, they needed quotes from him for click-bait fodder and to promote their "counter-narratives."

### "KKKroll Must Go!"

So, when Bob decided to ignore the media, people lost their minds. "KKKroll Must Go!" and "Fire Bob KKKroll" showed up on t-shirts, protest signs, and practically everywhere on social media. As a public figure and union leader, Bob was used to criticism. Although, this soon led to outright lies and unchecked outrage. Even some of Bob's friends and former allies turned against him for a chance in the media spotlight. For example, former MPD Chief Janeé Harteau came out of the woodwork and suddenly became one of Bob's harshest critics. Of course, she criticized him while complimenting herself when she tweeted:[92]

> "They elected him out of fear. A fear created over many years, but one that has been cultivated by him while we worked hard to take progressive police reform since Ferguson."

---

92. Harteau, J. [@ChiefHarteau]. (2020, June 1). *A disgrace to the badge! This is the battle that myself and others have been fighting against [...]* [Tweet] Twitter. https://twitter.com/ChiefHarteau/status/1267460683408564225

Harteau's comments seemed like revisionist history. Bob and Harteau got along fine, even long before she became chief. They were both in episodes of *COPS* back in the day (Harteau could be seen roughing up a drunk guy and playing drums, while Bob's mustache made its television debut). More recently, in 2017, they negotiated a long-overdue police contract. The *Star Tribune* quoted Harteau saying everyone worked "very hard in good faith to find common ground, which I believe will allow the MPD to serve its residents more effectively and more efficiently."[93] She didn't say anything about fear or lack of reform. But after the riots, she said Bob had been fearmongering and obstructing "reform." In response to a letter Bob wrote to union members, Harteau boldly stated that he was "tarnishing the badge of every cop in the United States."[94] She also said:[95]

> "This is the battle that myself and others have been fighting against. Bob Kroll turn in your badge!"

Funny, she didn't seem to be "fighting" with Bob back then, even during contract negotiations. If anyone in the media did any fact-checking, Harteau would have plenty of explaining to do. If a picture is worth a thousand words, then a photo taken after contract negotiations had finished says everything about her claims of "fear" and "fighting" for progress.

---

93. Jany, L. (2017, February 27). City of Minneapolis, police officers reach tentative contract deal. *Star Tribune.*

94. Harteau: Kroll's silence is just as much and just as important and loud as those who blatantly do racist things. (2020, June 1). *The Chad Hartman Show, WCCO News Talk 830.*

95. Ex-Minneapolis police chief to police union president: "Turn in your badge." (2020, June 1). *Fox 9 KMSP.*

*Minneapolis Police Chief Janeé Harteau and Lt. Bob Kroll, president of the Police Officers Federation of Minneapolis after contract negotiations in February 2017. (Photo courtesy of Bob Kroll).*

## Becoming Eva Braun

The media and the Left went wild over Harteau's attacks against Bob. It was precisely the anti-cop "counter-narrative" they were after, and from a minority woman no less. Of course, WCCO published an article about it. But when they did, they included a "conflict of interest" disclaimer:[96]

> "'This is the battle that myself and others have been fighting against. Bob Kroll turn in your badge!' Harteau said.
>
> WCCO-TV anchor/reporter Liz Collin is married to Bob Kroll. To avoid any potential conflict of interest, Liz has not reported on Minneapolis Police and Minneapolis Police Union issues for at least two-and-a-half years."

The fact that someone was criticizing Bob was hardly anything new. But seeing WCCO put a disclaimer about me—one of their own news reporters—was a bit unexpected. Of course, I could understand the situation and the optics. But putting a disclaimer about me in every story about Bob seemed suspicious. Since they were pushing their anti-cop rhetoric and weren't saying anything positive, it also seemed defamatory. Their disclaimers were damaging my reputation—and it seemed like they were using them to push me out of my job, if not the news industry. Unfortunately, they also led to dangerous consequences.

Before May 25, 2020, our marriage wasn't controversial. But now that Bob was a scapegoat and somehow responsible for George Floyd's death and the riots, I was also somehow responsible. Since the media and the Left started attacking Bob personally, they also started attacking me. For example, Rachelle Thorpe started a change.org petition titled: "WCCO: Ask Liz Collins [sic] to Step

---

96. MPD union leader releases letter to officers critical of Minneapolis leadership. (2020, June 1). *WCCO*.

Down Due to White Supremacy Ties."[97] People were also making all kinds of racist accusations about me on social media. Some, like Billy Anderson (@BillyAn23338604), tweeted statements that clearly show their confused associations:[98]

> "The riots are all a result of Bob Kroll's leadership of the Mpls Police Federation. Liz Collin must be a racist too. because ex mayor [sic] Ryback calls Bob Kroll a racist Get that Collin bitch off the air forever."

Maybe I was too focused on my work or too naïve. I just never imagined that people would attack me, or my professionalism based on wokeness and their warped sense of reality. However, long before Bob and I were married, even before I decided to go on a date with him, I told my news director that I wanted to avoid stories about the police union. Integrity and telling the truth were important to me long before any of this happened. Even though I never said a word about George Floyd or the riots on the news, every bit of respect I earned in my twenty-year career was cast aside. I was blacklisted. I went from being a familiar face on WCCO-TV down to being on the news barely a minute a day. Ironically, with all the demands for "justice" against racism, I was labelled the "KKK queen," "Nazi Barbi," or "Eva Braun" (the wife of Adolf Hitler) and so many other vile things. These weren't just Twitter trolls. Prominent leaders, respected professionals, even God-fearing women like myself were attacking me.

---

97. Thorpe, R. (June 2020). WCCO: Ask Liz Collins [sic] to step down due to white supremacy ties. *Change.org.* https://www.change.org/p/wcco-wcco-ask-liz-collin-to-step-down-due-to-white-supremacy-ties

98. Anderson, B. [@BillyAn23338604] (2020, May, 30). *The riots are all a result of Bob Kroll's leadership of the Mpls police federation [...]* [Tweet] Twitter. https://twitter.com/BillyAn23338604/status/1266788866427584516

Take for example, Michele Manion, a co-founder of a non-profit foundation in Minnesota. While she was attacking Bob on social media, she also said:[99]

> "His wife, @lizcollin, is an anchor at the CBS affiliate in town, @WCCO. People around here call her Eva Braun."

Nobody ever called me Eva Braun before. But since she committed suicide after marrying Hitler, I'm not sure what Michelle was suggesting, but her name-calling seemed disturbing. This kind of hate, from people who were supposedly against racism and fascism, only became worse.

## Media Harassment

Bob was to blame for racism and the riots, so reporters were hounding him— actually, they were relentless. Some of the worst rioting in US history had just taken place, so there were far more pressing stories to cover. But for whatever reason, the media seemed obsessed with Bob. On June 2nd, about a week after the riots started, someone from the police unit monitoring the death threats against us called Bob with some disturbing news. Our home address was being blasted all over social media. Bob endured plenty of bad publicity and name-calling in the past. But thanks to the riots, the hate on social media was becoming more violent. The death threats were also becoming more serious. And now that our home address was all over social media, we didn't know what to expect. Within just a couple of hours, someone was knocking on our front door. Given the circumstances, we weren't expecting company. He just kept knocking and ringing the doorbell. Even our lazy dog jumped into guard-dog mode. After several minutes of barking and commotion, the guy went back to his car and left.

---

99. Manion, M. [@Mickee7] (2020, May 31). *His wife @lizcollin, is an anchor at the CBS affiliate in two, @WCCO. People around here call her Eva Braun* [Tweet] Twitter. https://twitter.com/Mickee7/status/1267161540186255361.

We had no idea who he was and why he was at our house. A sheriff's deputy saw the guy driving around our neighborhood and stopped him to investigate. The guy said he came to our house to ask questions and demand answers from Bob.[100] He wasn't wearing a media badge or press ID, but said he was a reporter from *The Washington Post*. Apparently, members of the press were no longer taking "no comment" for an answer. I'd like to think that a national publication like *The Washington Post* wasn't asking their reporters to ambush fellow reporters and their spouses at home. Aside from his lack of professionalism, the articles he wrote before the riots were mostly about sports and COVID. So maybe he was just another overnight journalist-turned-activist fixated on attacking Bob.

**The Protests Outside WCCO**

The next day, June 3rd, the hateful accusations against Bob and I started boiling over. That's the day when former officers Kueng, Lane, and Thao were charged with aiding and abetting in the "murder" of George Floyd. Each of them was arrested and held on $1 million bail.[101] The charges against former officer Derek Chauvin were elevated from third-degree murder to second-degree murder. Supposedly, the demands for "justice" were about arresting and charging all four of the officers. Apparently, that wasn't enough because BLM protesters were still planning to hold a rally outside WCCO to demand my termination. Obviously, this wasn't about justice. The fact that a civil rights attorney, Nekima Levy Armstrong, was helping to organize the protest against me seemed ridiculous. Levy Armstrong was supposedly against racism. After all, she spoke out against the photo of a t-shirt Kim Voss shared on social

---

100. This incident was briefly mentioned in the following article: Shammas, B., Bellware, K., & Dennis, B. (2020, June 3). Murder charges filed against all four officers in George Floyd's death as protests against biased policing continue. *The Washington Post*. See also, Bob Kroll called police on Washington Post reporter who knocked on his door. (2020, June 6). *Bring Me The News*.

101. O'Brien, B. (2020, June 4). Bail set at $1 million for three former Minneapolis police officers charged in Floyd case. *Reuters*.

media. Levy Armstrong claimed to be about *civil* rights. I know because I've interviewed her several times. So, it seemed strange that she was referring to the "KKK" in calling Bob "KKKroll." She also didn't seem to mind using the same childish naming-calling in her defamatory Twitter posts telling others to protest against me:[102]

> "Breaking: All four cops who killed #GeorgeFloyd have been charged! Chauvin was charged with 2nd Degree murder. Other three cops have been charged with aiding and abetting. Protest is still on at 4pm today at WCCO TV, where Bob KKKroll's wife works. Be there."

What may have started in the name of "justice" apparently devolved into mob rule and identity politics. As if I didn't have my own career, or my own political perspectives, and my own opinions, it seemed that anyone in law enforcement—or anyone married to a police officer—had to be cancelled. Surprisingly, WCCO management seemed more concerned about making sure protesters had plenty of bottled water. Even though the windows were still boarded up from the rioting, it never occurred to them that water bottles were handy projectiles. After being reminded about the rioting the week before, they realized passing out projectiles was probably not a good idea. The protest started off with organizers demanding accountability from the media. That's something I agree with, even though it might be for different reasons. But then they started insulting me personally—for the color of my hair and skin. They were also calling Bob names and shouting about how he was supposedly President Trump's "number one supporter in Minnesota."[103] Since they couldn't get in front of Trump, I guess Bob was a stand-in they could assail with their race-based rhetoric. Meanwhile, I was working on the most

---

102. Levy Armstrong, N. [@nvlevy]. (2020, June 3). *Breaking: All four cops who killed #GeorgeFloyd have been charged [...]* [Tweet] Twitter. Deleted.

103. Unicorn Riot. (2020, June 3). *Action at WCCO to end media bias against victims of police violence: Day 9* [Video]. YouTube. https://youtu.be/oPXL0erntYo

ridiculous assignment I've ever had. My news director asked me to put together a list of all the "important" stories I've done. For whatever reason, I now had to defend myself and my career as if I were guilty of something.

Looking around the WCCO newsroom, there was Esme Murphy. She famously declared Hillary Clinton the winner of the 2016 presidential election and constantly celebrated democrats and progressive politicians in the newsroom. But despite her obvious bias, WCCO didn't stop her from anchoring and reporting on politics.

There was also Caroline Lowe. She was a crime reporter for WCCO and respectably worked as a Minnesota State Fair Police officer for years. But WCCO didn't stop her from reporting about crime and the police.

And then there was Kate Raddatz. She previously dated Jacob Frey. But WCCO didn't stop her from regularly reporting about him, his role as the mayor of Minneapolis, or the city government.

So much for avoiding media bias. None of the accusations against me made sense *professionally*, but I guess they did *politically*. Maybe, the accusations had more to do with Bob questioning the narrative that the media and the Left were desperately trying to control. Maybe they didn't like that Bob was demanding the body cam footage and refusing to ignore Floyd's criminal past. Or maybe they didn't like that he was calling out how Frey and Arradondo abandoned police officers and everybody else in Minneapolis during the riots.

The support I received from family and friends was about the only good that came out of all this. People who watched me over the years on TV were truly kind—their kindness kept me going when I needed it the most. Strangers were openly supportive and were even sticking up for me on social media. Some people in the WCCO newsroom were supportive but said they couldn't show their support in public because they were afraid of being cancelled. Bob and I understood their situation. But maybe that was part of the problem. Admittedly, I should have recognized how cancel culture and mob mentality were profoundly changing how we treat one another—and I should have done more to speak out.

## Promising "Change" and Police Reform?

Before May 25, 2020, "reforming" the Minneapolis Police Department was hardly an urgent priority for city leaders. It certainly wasn't a top story constantly in the news, either. Frey claimed to be all about police reform but seemed more concerned with regulating off-duty police work and moonlighting.[104] The media and the Left were apparently still obsessed with conspiracies about Bob attending a Trump rally. For example, Libor Jany, a reporter for the *Star Tribune* claimed that "Trump's embrace of Kroll seems to be part of a broader GOP strategy to make urban crime a campaign issue in 2020."[105] So, the fact that Bob or the police union had been obstructing "change" hardly seemed like an issue.

All that changed overnight when protesters started demanding "justice" and police reform. In response, the city council announced it was going to "defund" the police department. To avoid being left behind and left with the blame, Frey apparently needed to make a bold move of his own. On June 10th, Mayor Frey and Chief Arradondo held a press conference. Anticipating a big development in the investigation, it was going to be broadcast live on national television. Instead, Arradondo simply announced that he was no longer participating in contract negotiations with the police union. However, Arradondo did say a few things about race:

---

104. Nesternak, M. (2020, January 31). Mayor Frey aims to rein in off-duty police work, creates task force. *Minnesota Reformer*.

105. Jany, L. (2019, November 3). Amid attention and controversy, Minneapolis police union head has no regrets. *Star Tribune*.

"History is being written now and I'm determined to make sure we are on the right side of history...

Race is inextricably part of the American policing system. We will never evolve in this profession if we do not address it head on... Communities of color have paid the heaviest of costs, and that is with their lives."

Mayor Frey applauded Arradondo's "decision." He also dodged accountability—and scapegoated Bob—during the press conference:[106]

"Lieutenant Kroll has not been helpful in any way, shape or form to generating accountability, and measures of reform that we've been trying to see through."

Anyone who was barely paying attention could've noticed that Frey and Arradondo didn't mention any specific reforms they were trying to make *before* the riots—but were just making promises for the future. The hypocrisy also seemed obvious. The riots and the alleged worst act of "police racism" in America happened under Mayor Frey's command. Frey was not only sidestepping accountability, but he was also trying to eliminate his lack of leadership from the equation and pining his failures on Bob and the police union. The press conference seemed like comedy hour when Frey apparently started talking in circles as he continued blaming Bob:[107]

"For someone that complains so much about a lack of support and trust of police officers, he's one of the primary reasons for that lack of trust and support."

Frey might have made himself dizzy with all that circular reasoning because he didn't seem to realize that walking away from contract negotiations only

106. Olson, R. (2020, June 10). Frey backs MPD chief's move on police union negotiations, believes it can bring change. *Fox 9 KMSP*.

107. Minneapolis Police Department is withdrawing from union contract negotiations, chief says. (2020, June 11). *WCCO/CBS News*.

proved Bob's point. However, if Frey or the media were paying any attention, they would have noticed that Bob wasn't even part of the contract negotiating team. Nonetheless, the chief and mayor were abandoning police officers once again at the worst possible moment. Along with working 12-hour shifts, recovering from their injuries, and trying to put the riots behind them, officers now had to worry about the uncertainty of their wages and benefits.

## Blaming Cops—But Not Arradondo

The media and the Left celebrated the PR move that Frey and Arradondo were symbolically making. At the same time, they went out of their way not to blame Frey or Arradondo for anything. City council member Jeremiah Ellison made it obvious when he said:[108]

> "I think the reason we're going this route is because the leadership in the MPD, and by leadership, I don't mean Rondo... I mean the union leadership has made it clear they're not going to be held accountable. They're going to resist accountability."

## Police Reform without Body Cameras?

Maybe I'm biased. I mean, that's what the protesters were claiming. So, let's say Bob *was* the roadblock for police accountability and reforms. Even if that were possible, Frey and Arradondo were still obstructing reform themselves. They were obstructing the single most important police reform in America[109]— the one protesters and reformers have been demanding since the riots in Ferguson: they were still refusing to release the body cam videos. Ironically,

---

108. Olson, R. (2020, June 10). Frey backs MPD chief's move on police union negotiations, believes it can bring change. *Fox 9 KMSP.*

109. Berman, M. (2015, May 1). Justice Dept. will spend $20 million on police body cameras nationwide. *The Washington Post.*

Bob was demanding their release even before the riots started. If Frey and Arradondo were so concerned about reform, they would have released them.

## The More Things "Reform," The More They Stay the Same

Arradondo seemed to be taking a bold step toward defunding the police department. Although, in reality, he was the only one walking away from the table. His deputy chiefs along with other city officials would still be negotiating with the union. They even had a meeting scheduled for August, so it wasn't like negotiations completely stopped. They later cancelled the meeting because they couldn't figure out who would make decisions if Arradondo wasn't there. After Bob retired in January 2021, Arradondo started attending the meetings again. But the most absurd thing about this political move is that Frey and Arradondo promised to make sweeping changes and reforms. However, they basically agreed to the same contract that was in place before they symbolically walked away. The city council, whose members defiantly proclaimed to "defund the police," passed the contract—which now included bonuses for police officers—with an overwhelming 8 to 5 vote.[110]

## Arradondo, The Cop Who Refused to Carry a Gun

Withdrawing from negotiations with the police union helped Chief Arradondo and Mayor Frey hide their failures and look like heroes. It apparently helped them avoid the wrath of delusional protesters seeking to defund the police. It also sent a clear message to Bob, personally and professionally. Behind their promises and picture-perfect press conferences, it was clear to Bob that support he gave to Arradondo was no longer mutual. But even more significantly, Arradondo was turning his back on the police union, the same union that saved his job and his career.

---

110. McLaughlin, S. (2022, March 24). Minneapolis City Council approves new police contract: Officer bonuses, no changes in discipline. *Bring Me The News*.

Sometime in the late '90s, Arradondo, or another detective who looked a lot like him, was at a local bank when someone came in to rob it. It was like something out of a Hollywood movie when the hero cop foils a bank robbery and saves the day—except none of that actually happened. Someone inside the bank tripped the silent alarm. A different cop, who was nearby, rushed to the scene, because that's what cops do. The robber ran out of the back. But the detective who was inside the bank—and didn't take any action—quietly slipped out the front. Everyone on the department was convinced it was Arradondo. He certainly matched the description and he was also the only cop on the Minneapolis Police Department who refused to carry a gun.

Shortly after the bank robbery, Chief Olson wanted to fire Arradondo. Al Berryman, the president of the police union at the time, persuaded Olson not to fire him. Arradondo claimed that it was against his religion to carry a gun. But as Berryman argued on his behalf, back then you could walk into Room 108, where all the sergeants in the detective division worked, and find plenty of empty holsters and plenty of guns in desk drawers. Even though Arradondo's refusal to carry a gun went against department policy, firing him wouldn't have been fair. Chief Olson reluctantly agreed and decided not to fire him. Instead, he gave Arradondo another assignment and time to think about his beliefs and his career. Weeks later, Arradondo chose his career and carrying a gun. Not long after that, Arradondo was promoted, and kept on getting promoted until he became Chief of the Minneapolis Police Department. There's no way he could have forgotten how the union stood up for him and saved his job. So, with all that in mind, Arradondo wasn't just turning his back on negotiations, he was turning his back on the union, and some of the very same people who fought to give him a second chance. For Bob, it was even more personal. No matter how complicated a situation might have been, Bob and Arradondo always shared mutual respect and understanding. They always found common ground to do what was best for the city, the citizens, and the police officers sworn to protect them. Arradondo was turning away from that sense of fairness that was Al Berryman's legacy (which influenced Bob since he was a rookie cop) and saved Arradondo's career.

## Protesters Outside Our House

Frey and Arradondo weren't the only ones holding symbolic press conferences. Governor Walz held a press conference urging the importance of "creating space" for "peaceful protesters." Walz and Lieutenant Governor Flanagan let rioting and looting go on for days but seemed clueless about the damage the "peaceful" protesting had caused. They didn't seem to understand that people needed strong leadership not symbolic gestures. The way that Walz, Flanagan, Frey, and Arradondo were scapegoating cops was like putting a target on the back of every law enforcement officer in Minnesota. So, when they started blaming Bob for racism and the riots, they not only made him a target, they also made him Public Enemy No. 1.

Like all the violence and incivility that the media and the Left promoted during the riots, the attacks against Bob quickly escalated while common sense seemed to disappear. Just days later after Arradondo and Frey made their "defund the police" contract maneuver, BLM protesters held a demonstration at our house. On June 14, 2020, Black Lives Matter and Black Trans Lives Matter protesters, held signs and wrote messages in sidewalk chalk in front of our house. "Bob Kroll is a racist" was a popular theme. If their scribbles were meant to be political statements, apparently Bob was also responsible for "400 years of racial injustice" and other confused ideas. Fortunately, it was little more than insults, sidewalk chalk, and a mural of George Floyd stuck on the side of a rented moving van. But more than anything else, it was now perfectly clear that Bob was to blame for everything.

Even though they completely violated our privacy, at least they showed *some* respect for our property. Although I didn't know what to say to our neighbors.

They did nothing to deserve the chanting, the obscene messages, and everything else that happened outside their homes. But they were absolutely amazing. As soon as the protesters drove off, our neighbors came out and cleaned up the mess. They washed away all the hurtful messages that "Bob Kroll must see!" We came home to find our driveway filled with hearts drawn with sidewalk chalk and messages of encouragement. It's still hard to put into words how the kindness and support of our neighbors helped us. They gave us hope. And if our neighbors were standing up to the nonsense, then Bob and I had to do the same. Little did I know this was just the beginning because it didn't take long for violence to show up at our house. Our political "leaders" should have realized that "defunding" the police, abandoning union members, and blaming police officers might lead to dire consequences. The statement Arradondo released on June 22nd seemed to only make things worse:[111]

> "I agree with Attorney General Ellison: what happened to Mr. Floyd was murder."

Arradondo seemed to be reading a death sentence in the court of public opinion. His indictment wasn't something a leader should say to calm a situation. When Derek Chauvin heard about Arradondo's public indictment, he said, "That's when I knew they were stacking the deck against me."[112]

## Death Threats & A Bomb Threat in the Mail

Two months after the riots, Bob and I were getting used to hateful attacks and death threats. However, on July 24th, I noticed an envelope in the mail that seemed a little odd. As soon as I opened it, I wished I never did.

---

111. Minneapolis Police Chief on George Floyd Death: 'This was murder—it wasn't a lack of training.' (2020, June 22). *Fox 9 KMSP*.
112. D. Chauvin (personal communication, August 16, 2022).

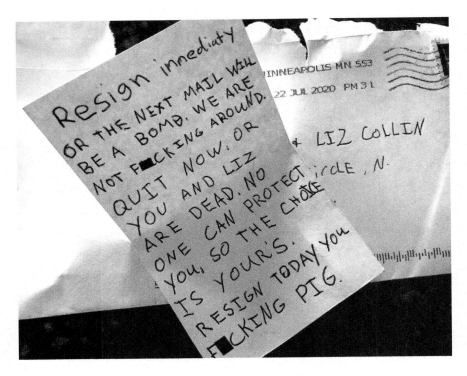

*Death threat that Bob and I received in the mail on July 24, 2020; censored.*

Of course, Bob was out of town that day. But like a former SWAT team leader, when I called him, he walked me through the protocols. I called the county sheriff's office to file a report. They went above and beyond; they took the letter and tested it for fingerprints and other evidence. While I wanted them to arrest whoever did this, I doubted that would ever happen. So, Bob and I were surprised when the sheriff's office called us back—they identified someone. Fingerprints on the letter matched those of a suspect arrested for throwing a bottle at a police officer during a protest in Oregon. His name was Jacob Pierre Boucher. He eventually pled guilty in federal court to "mailing threatening communications" and was sentenced to 10 days in federal prison.[113] But from

113. United States of America v. Jacob Pierre Boucher, 0:21-CR-00184-PSJ(1); USM No. 65201-509.

the day we received his threatening letter, even checking the mail became an ordeal—and something I could never let my seven-year-old son do anymore. He couldn't comprehend what was going on that summer, especially since we had to rush and shuffle him around so many times just to keep him safe.

## BLM Comes Back to Hugo

August 15, 2020 is a day I don't think I'll ever forget. It brought out extraordinary acts of courage and humanity. It also revealed some of the most despicable acts of incivility and ignorance by the media and the Left I have ever seen. Admittedly, I have a unique perspective since this happened at my own house—and the cover-ups happened in my own newsroom. Nekima Levy Armstrong, yes *that* Nekima Levy Armstrong—the civil-rights attorney, former law professor, and former candidate for the mayor of Minneapolis—and her Racial Justice Network organized a protest outside our house that day. Levy Armstrong shared her opening "remarks" with the crowd:[114]

> "Liz Collin has used her white power and her white privilege on WCCO, which is an affiliate of CBS, and shame on CBS, because instead of holding Liz Collin accountable and firing her for her lack of journalistic ethics and integrity, they gave Bob Kroll a platform in the aftermath of George Kroll—George Floyd being killed. So, shame on WCCO. Shame on Liz Collin. Shame on CBS. Because all they do is empower people like Bob Kroll to keep doing what he's doing which is terrorizing people in the city of Minneapolis and thinking that he can get away with it. But we're not going to rest until Bob Kroll's raggedy ass gets fired. Period. Point. Blank. And then the sad part, I see a dog down the street barking, I'm like damn, ya'll done trained your dogs to be racist? I mean, c'mon ya'll that's absolutely ridiculous."

---

114. Unicorn Riot. (2020, August 15). *Protest from outside the house of Bob Kroll, president of the Minneapolis Police union* [Video]. YouTube. https://youtu.be/GsEeYFDlKXc

Levy Armstrong then introduced John Thompson, a candidate for the Minnesota House of Representatives. Instead of anything that resembles diplomacy or anything we should expect of an elected legislator, Thompson launched into a deranged tirade:

> "Oh man, hey I was standing over here burning up because I was telling Marquis somebody got to tell these white people out here that there was a public hanging in Duluth, Minnesota and there was an audience... and the audience had grandkids."

> [Shouting at our neighbors] "And there they go, over there, you know, come on back out with your "Blue Lives Matter" shirt. And I mean that. Let me tell you about Blue Lives Matter all right, because they didn't come out with Blue Lives Matter 'til we start saying Black Lives Matter. But unlike you, white man, you can unzip that f-cking costume! I can't unzip this black skin I'm in! I'm a black man being terrorized by this f-cking Klansman right here! We are terrorized by the grand wizard!"

> [Pointing to our house] "Y'all got the grand wizard living in your goddamn neighborhood! All the Klan exists in Hugo, Minnesota and it's right here!"

> [Screaming at our neighbors] "Don't run now don't run now racist white people! I'm here! Oh yeah, we pull up! We pull the f-ck up! And we here! Come on over here with your Blue Lives Matter shirt! Blue lives ain't shit! And if people in Hugo don't support black people, f-ck Hugo Minnesota! Now we can get to what I was talking about. You right, you right, I did, I won the primary election and y'all can quote, quote me on this, I am going to the state capitol with this same f-cking message that black people are tired of being killed in these f-cking streets and ya'll people defending this shit! Listen when I tell y'all, the K-K-K ain't never left the state of Minnesota. As a matter of fact we in Klan land right now!"

[Shouting at our neighbor's daughters] "Now y'all run your coward ass in the damn garage! C'm on out here! C'mon out here, say something, white racist motherf-ckers!"

[Applause]

"Ain't nobody gonna sugarcoat racism! Wa'n't nothin' pretty about Bob Kroll kicking that 15-year-old boy in his face![115] So why the fuck is we so peaceful in this raggedy-ass neighborhood? F-ck ya'll your motherf-cking peace, white racist mother-ckers! Shouldn't gave me the microphone! Shouldn't gave me the f-cking microphone."

[Screaming at neighbors with Blue Lives Matter Flag] "You coward ass, standing way the f-ck back there with your Blue Lives Matter shirt, I can't unzip this goddamn black skin on me! "You can take that sign and stick it in yo ass!"

"Yeah, they ain't never seen a legislator like this before. Now back to what I was saying. We coming. We coming for everything that you motherf-ckers took from us. We coming for them seats! We coming for the money you owe us! We coming for this—wait a minute! This whole goddamn state burned down for 20 goddamn dollars you think we give a f-ck about burning Hugo down?!"

[Shouting at our neighbors] "I know running your coward ass back in the garage... and changing shirts. Blue Lives don't mean shit to black people! Bro! Where he go? Tucson—they ain't never had to worry about the police pulling them over and putting them on the goddamn hood of they car and sticking their fingers in our ass looking for f-cking dope—and c'mon man! Have ya'll had to worry about that shit in Hugo?!"

---

115. State Representative-elect Thompson was apparently referring to a bogus complaint filed in the early 1990s. Bob Kroll was cleared of any wrongdoing.

[Yelling at our neighbors] "Have you had to worry about—don't hide your face Karen! Take that shit off yo face! The klan... don't hide your face Karen! Take that shit off your face! You're a coward. You're a coward—the klan used to wear masks. Now you wanna be one. I know what I'm talking about. This ain't rhetoric bro. I've been black all my life. I didn't come here to be peaceful and Hugo, and kum-ba-ya my Lord. F-ck Hugo Minnesota! F-ck Bob Kroll! And f-ck anybody who support his racist ass."

[Yelling at police security cameras] "Thank you Washington County for providing free coverage for this. F-ck Bob Kroll! I said it! And if you uphold racism, f-ck you too! We coming for what's ours. Y'all owe us!" Goddammit we paid for that shit! Them taxpayers dollars that paid for that shit. They came out our pockets. When they come to policing, we paid for that shit. Goddammit, y'all owe us a refund on our goddamn money! I'm tired of talking about it. I'm tired of marching about it. I'm tired of people saying we just protesters, so let's take our ass to the capitol! Let's take our ass to the motherf-cking mayor's office. Let's take our ass to the city council seat, to the school board. Let me tell y'all something about the school board. They used to beat us for learning, now they call that shit a motherf-cking achievement gap. I know what the f-ck I'm talking about cause my kid is black. They ain't gotta worry about that in Hugo Minnesota!"

[Applause]

"Any way they can oppress black people, they've done it. And we're just right here telling y'all we sick of it. We pullin' up. We pulling up to your house. We'll pull up to your house. And where this nigg— Washington County Sheriff over there, we'll pull up to your goddamn house too. We sick of y'all killing black people. And if y'all don't understand that we gonna pull up! Y'all supporting this bullshit and acting like racism don't exist here."

"I said it, and I say it again. Three black men were hung in Duluth. There was an audience watching these black men, cheering these people on when they was hanging these black men for something they did not do. Where the f-ck you think their grandkids went? Where do you think they nephews and the people that was in the crowd—they had kids. They moved here to Hugo, Minnesota. Brandon, Minnesota. Woodbury, Minnesota."

"Some of these cowards used to get their ass whooped in high school and now they got on the Blue Lives Matter shirt. F-ck blue lives. There's no such thing as a—show me a blue life. Show me a f-cking blue life. I cannot unzip this costume I'm in, I promise y'all. I've been black all my life. I can't scrape this toast off my skin. But these cowards in these blue uniforms they can take that shit off and go back to being regular people shopping in our stores, making money off our goddamn tax dollars!"

"I'm glad y'all making them uncomfortable here in Hugo, Minnesota. God damn it we'll pull up to Duluth, Minnesota! We'll pull up to Virginia, Minnesota. We pull up to [inaudible] in Minnesota! We tired of telling—we sick of y'all white ass treat us like shit and acting like we ain't comfortable with it. I'm not comfortable getting my ass kicked by you coward-ass white motherf-ckers in uniform and if you uncomfortable with my voice, do something about it."

"Oh, they ain't never seen a legislator like this before y'all. I'm not Bobby Joe—I'm not, I'm not none of them—a shout out to the brothers—but I'm not that motherf-cker to come and sugarcoat racism, ya'll. I'm not about to come here—I didn't come to play with y'all. I didn't come to say oh my God, we must—f-ck overcoming. We didn't overcame 400 years of bullshit. We not over—we're not gonna reimagine shit no more. We gonna make this shit reality. Y'all didn't think we was coming to Hugo. Here we are."

[Again, yelling at police security cameras] "Thank you for the aerial coverage and please tell Bob Kroll, I know you're watching live, f-ck you! F-ck this house and f-ck the racist-ass Minneapolis police officers that keep [inaudible] our goddamn community! I love y'all."

## When Civil-Rights Attorney Levy Armstrong Called Bob a "C-nt"

Nekima Levy Armstrong then took the microphone seeking praise for Thompson:

"Let's give it up for John Thompson! Like he said, you ain't never seen a legislator like this before."

She then led protesters in a march around our neighborhood. Afterward, she still wasn't quite finished yet and shared a few "choice" words of her own. Levy Armstrong separated the Black protesters from everyone else and invited them on to our front lawn:

"I want the Black people who are here to go over to that flagpole [the one in our front yard], because wouldn't you know it, he [Bob] got an American flag."

So, we gonna take a knee right outside Bob Kroll's house and in the spirit of Colin Kapernick, who was standing up for Black people who've been slain by the police—so if you are Black and you are at this protest come on over to this flagpole so we can take a knee."

"Allies let's stand in solidarity with support. Let's cheer on our Black folks, who courageously... Stand up against that cowardly c-nt Bob Kroll..."

"So, we gonna kneel right outside the flagpole of his bitch-ass house and we gonna take a knee. C'mon Black folks!"

*(Top) Protesters kneeling on my front lawn during a protest, August 15, 2020. (Bottom) A protester bashing a piñata look-alike of me in my driveway. Images are screenshots from: Unicorn Riot (2020, August 15).* Protest from outside the house of Bob Kroll, president of the Minneapolis police union *[Video]. YouTube. https://youtu.be/GsEeYFDlKXc.*

*(Top) Protesters carrying piñatas of Bob and myself while marching through our neighborhood on August 15, 2020. (Bottom) State representative candidate John Thompson "speaking" with protesters outside our house. Images are screenshots from: Unicorn Riot (2020, August 15).* Protest from outside the house of Bob Kroll, president of the Minneapolis police union *[Video]. YouTube. https://youtu.be/GsEeYFDlKXc.*

## Levy Armstrong—Oprah's Idea of a "Force for Good?"

Levy Armstrong then told the protesters to leave their signs in our driveway. The protesters hesitated at first, but then she encouraged the crowd by saying:

> "Don't be scared, f-ck Bob Kroll [...] he and Liz Collin can pick that shit up."

After all, as the protest organizer, Levy Armstrong was telling others what to do and where to go, while getting attention for herself. Speaking of getting attention, several months later Oprah interviewed Levy Armstrong about her "fight for racial justice."[116] Oprah praised her for organizing one of "the first protests in Floyd's name." However, Levy Armstrong didn't mention how she also helped organize the first protest outside WCCO where I worked—and another one outside my house. Although, she did tell Oprah that after George Floyd was arrested and died, she felt the "need to bring people together as soon as possible." But Levy Armstrong didn't mention that she segregated Black people and told them to kneel on our front lawn to disrespect the American flag. She also didn't mention that she was the first person to praise and seek applause for John Thompson after his violent and vulgar rant outside our house.

Oprah has been encouraging her fans to "be a force for good."[117] So it's hard to imagine how Oprah thinks Levy Armstrong fits that profile considering her vulgar, race-obsessed remarks—and how she gave a hate-spewing politician like Thompson a welcoming platform during a protest outside the home of a female TV news reporter. I know this isn't all about me. But it's difficult to understand how Oprah could simply overlook Levy Armstrong's questionable behavior, especially when it was live-streamed and widely available on social

---

116. Nicolaou, E. (2021, April 21). Oprah asks activist Nekima Levy Armstrong "Where do we go from here?" After Chauvin verdict," *Oprah Daily*.

117. Vassar, L. (2020, October 29). Oprah Winfrey wants OWN to be a "force for good." *Essence*.

media. The way Oprah expressed her gratitude for Levy Armstrong by quoting US representative John Lewis—a true civil-rights leader—by saying, "thank you for your good trouble" seemed almost blasphemous.

## WCCO: Hiding Information & Helping John Thompson

By now it was practically impossible to keep track of who was lying to whom. Even Thompson was apparently lying to himself and everyone else who was watching his tirade on social media. Bob ran into him just a few months before all of this. Thompson said "Hey, how are you, good to see you" or something like that—it was hardly confrontational. That's probably because he knew that Bob grew up on the East side of St. Paul in a Democrat household near the district Thompson was seeking to represent. This made Thompson's hate-spewing "speech" in front of our house seem even more like self-serving performance art. Aside from Thompson's vulgarities, the way that WCCO handled it said everything about their priorities. They basically did nothing. Just to be clear, a WCCO news anchor was harassed on social media. BLM supporters held a protest outside WCCO. They held a protest at her house. She received death threats in the mail that led to a conviction in federal court. Thompson, a candidate for state representative, shouted violent threats and bashed a piñata that looked like her in her own driveway, where protesters left behind piles of insulting signs during yet another protest at her house. Except for sending out an email days after one of the first protests, and finally mentioning it on the news, WCCO didn't do much else.

In stark contrast, about two months later, a WCCO photojournalist had his phone knocked out of his hand by a 70-year-old man at a Trump rally. As WCCO quickly reported, the photographer "was not harmed in the attack, nor was his phone broken."[118] Since the man was wearing a pro-Trump t-shirt, it

---

118. WCCO photojournalist moving forward with charges against man who punched phone out of his hand. (2020, October 6). *WCCO/CBS Minnesota*.

seemed like WCCO management had to take immediate action. They made sure a police report was filed and offered to support the photographer throughout the "ordeal." They also covered the story for months in several WCCO articles and interviews—even a promotional campaign. The difference between the way WCCO handled the protests and violent threats involving protesters wearing BLM t-shirts against a news reporter—and a 70-year-old man wearing a Trump t-shirt who smacked a phone out of a photographer's hand—isn't necessarily the issue. The deep-rooted media bias that led WCCO and so many other networks to take sides and manipulate the "truth" is profoundly more concerning.

Thompson's tirade outside our house speaks for itself. His fellow members of the Minnesota DFL pretended to publicly scold him, but still endorsed him. With their help and support, Thompson won the election in November 2020. Thompson also had some inside help from WCCO and most likely other news and media outlets. In October 2020, about two months after the protest at our house, WCCO received information about Thompson's criminal history and sordid past. It referenced his involvement in more than a few criminal allegations and his eligibility for election. All the information could have been verified, but for whatever reason, WCCO ignored it.

That's the problem: ignoring significant, verifiable information that seriously questions the integrity of a political candidate defies everything people should expect with regard to ethical news reporting. I tried telling my news director that I get it; reporting about the protest at my house and Thompson's involvement could have been a public relations disaster. But ignoring Thompson's apparent history of making threats and committing violence against women—and withholding it during an upcoming election—was simply wrong. I was trying to be diplomatic, but my boss turned it into another "Liz, please spare me your speech on journalist integrity" moments.

More than anything else, this proved to me that WCCO had now become far more concerned with being a political platform for the Left. Withholding information to help a candidate win an election underscored just how far bias had crept into the newsroom. WCCO always leaned to the left, which was fine. I worked there for years and was well aware of the fact. Besides, there isn't a newsroom in America that doesn't lean toward one party or another. But when political bias becomes *the* reason for ignoring facts and manipulating the news, there's a problem. Protesters stood on my front lawn shaming me because of my alleged bias, yet my boss was telling me to shut up about journalistic integrity. Since you're reading this, I obviously refused to be silenced.

**Thompson Was Kicked Out of the Party, But Not Out of the House**

Thompson's past caught up to him in July 2021. His past arrests for domestic violence, his guilty conviction for obstructing justice, a controversial traffic stop that drew attention to whether he was a Wisconsin resident while representing a district in Minnesota, and calling a fellow house representative a "racist," finally seemed to be too much for even the Left and WCCO to ignore. Thompson was expelled from the democratic party. His controversies were coming to light, so now it was politically important to help the DFL distance themselves. Since it no longer seemed to be necessary to conceal the information about Thompson, WCCO finally decided it was the time to call attention to it. One of my fellow anchors, Esme Murphy, shared the information on social media. People, like Brainerd city council member Gabe Johnson, noticed the date on the documents (10/16/2020) and realized WCCO had them for months.[119]

---

119. Johnson, G. [@THEGabeJohnson]. (2021, July 18). Did WCCO have these docs on 10/16/2020? [Tweet] Twitter. https://twitter.com/THEGabeJohnson/status/1416614116995653638

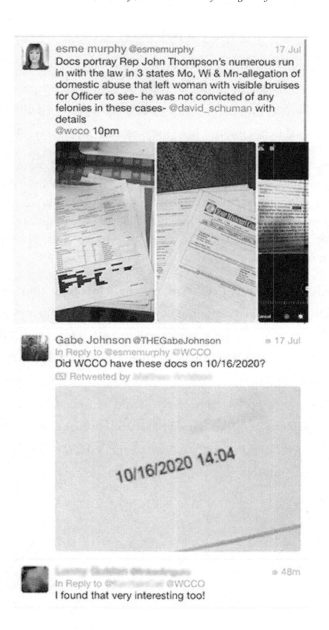

*Gabe Johnson questioning Esme Murphy and WCCO on Twitter about documents related to state representative John Thompson and his "numerous run in [sic] with the law" (Source: SingleSpeakMedia).*

Minnesota House Speaker Melissa Hortman previously failed to take action against Thompson. But now, she issued a joint statement with Majority Leader Ryan Winkler stating that it would be "best for Rep. Thompson, his family, and the institution for him to resign."[120] The DFL overlooked all of Thompson's less-than-dignified behavior, but now they quickly pointed out that:

> "Rep. Thompson's actions, credible reports of abuse and misconduct, and his failure to take responsibility remain unacceptable for a member of the Minnesota House of Representatives [...] In the absence of a resignation, the Minnesota House DFL has voted to remove Rep. Thompson from the caucus."

The statement from Hortman and Winkler says a lot about spin and "sugar-coating." Along with minimizing the wrongdoing of a democrat, the ousting of Thompson was just smoke and mirrors. Apparently, Thompson's behavior was making the DFL look bad, so to distance themselves, they kicked him out of the party. However, he was still a member of the Minnesota House of Representatives. Barring him completely would've forced democrats to vote against another democrat. That would have been unprecedented because the Minnesota House of Representatives hasn't expelled a member in more than 160 years, since Minnesota was a territory.

---

120. Coolican, J. P. (2021, September 14). Rep. John Thompson expelled from House DFL caucus. *Minnesota Reformer.*

# PART V

THE TRIAL OF DEREK CHAUVIN

The trial of the *State of Minnesota v. Derek Chauvin* started on March 8, 2021. Forty-three days later, on April 20th, the jury found Chauvin guilty on all three counts:

> Count I: Unintentional second-degree murder

> Count II: Third-degree murder

> Count III: Second-degree manslaughter

The verdict provided all the "proof" that's necessary for those who believe Derek Chauvin "murdered" George Floyd. But depending upon who you ask, the trial of Derek Chauvin was about more than justice for George Floyd. It was about long-overdue police accountability. It was also about righting wrongs of the past and dismantling "systemic police racism" for a better future.[121] However, the trial shouldn't have been about any of that. If the Bill of Rights and the Sixth Amendment still matter, then the trial should have been about evidence—and evidence alone. The Sixth Amendment grants everyone in America the right to a speedy trial by an *impartial* jury. Given all the things the trial was supposed to be about, it was everything but impartial. So many things about the trial can be debated, from the legion of prosecutors, to the "expert" witnesses, and everything in between. But putting aside all the symbolism and controversy—which is what a jury should do—there's one aspect that's been ignored. If there's any place to find impartiality, or the lack of it, it's in the jury instructions.

---

121. Forgrave, R., & Rao, M. (2021, March 28). Derek Chauvin trial represents a defining moment in America's racial history. *Star Tribune.*

## The Jury Instructions

The judge's instructions to the jury are supposed to make sure everything during a trial is done fairly. Most judges use pre-written texts and amend them as necessary depending upon the issues that arise during the trial.[122] Along with analogies about deer and deer tracks, Judge Cahill's instructions were a unique mix of standards and embellishments. Some of the instructions were straightforward. Others sounded like something out of George Orwell's dystopian book *1984*.[123] There were fourteen pages of instructions and going through them line by line would be a chore. But a brief look at some of them reveals how this trial was fundamentally flawed from the very beginning.

### Pay No Attention to the Protesters...

In giving instructions to the jury, Judge Cahill explained:[124]

> "It is your duty to decide the questions of fact in this case. It is my duty to give you the rules of law you must apply in arriving at your verdict."

Fair enough. But Judge Cahill also told the jury to do the impossible:

> "Deciding questions of fact is your exclusive responsibility. In doing so, you must consider all the evidence you have heard and seen in this trial, and *you must disregard anything you may have heard or seen elsewhere about this case.*"

With all the rioting in Minneapolis and elsewhere throughout the country, not to mention the murals of George Floyd, Governor Walz issuing a proclamation for a moment of silence to honor him, an act of Congress named after him,

---

122. See *Minnesota jury instruction guides, 2020-2021*. (2020). Minnesota District Judges Association Committee on Criminal Jury Instruction Guides, Thomson Reuters; Forestell, S. E. (2015). *Minnesota jury instruction guides, criminal*. Thomson Reuters.

123. Orwell, G. (1949). *Nineteen Eighty-four, A novel*. Harcourt, Brace and Company.

124. Cahill, J. (2021, April 19). *Jury instructions*. State of Minnesota v. Derek Chauvin, 27-CR-20-12646.

how could jurors simply disregard *anything* they've seen or heard? Even if they could ignore everything else, the barricades and protests outside the courthouse probably made impartiality more like an impossibility. The fact that they were partially sequestered and escorted into court every day by sheriff's deputies was also probably obvious.

**Demands for "Justice!" and the Presumption of Innocence?**

Regarding the presumption of innocence, which is supposed to be part of every jury trial, Judge Cahill told the jurors that Chauvin is presumed to be innocent until *proven* guilty beyond a reasonable doubt. In case anyone hadn't noticed somehow, Chauvin had already been found guilty long before his trial even started. As seen in the viral Facebook video, bystanders had sealed Chauvin's fate before the ambulance even arrived. Judge Cahill also told the jury that Chauvin was brought to trial before the court by *"ordinary* processes of the law."[125] But there's nothing "ordinary" about deliberating two murder charges and a manslaughter charge—related to the death of *one* person. With the charges stacked against him, there was hardly a sense of presumed innocence. The fact that Chauvin *had to be guilty* of something seemed more like the reality of the situation.

**Nothing Out of the Ordinary…**

Also, there was nothing "ordinary" about the development of Chauvin's trial. Instead of letting County Attorney Mike Freeman handle the prosecution, Governor Walz intervened just days after the riots started and designated Attorney General Keith Ellison as the lead prosecutor. There's nothing "ordinary" about that kind of decision. Walz also made things even worse when he explained that his decision was based upon a letter he received from state legislators. They were concerned because Freeman held a press

---

125. Cahill, J. (2021, April 19). *Jury instructions*. State of Minnesota v. Derek Chauvin, 27-CR-12646; emphasis added.

conference and said there was "exculpatory evidence that might exonerate the officers."[126] Freeman was the only prosecutor in the history of Minnesota to convict a police officer for murder. But in this case, he suggested there could be evidence to exonerate Chauvin. So, apparently, Walz had to give into demands and replace Freeman with the Antifa-supporting attorney general, Keith Ellison. Walz raised a few eyebrows in switching the lead prosecutors, especially since Ellison seemed to be quite proud of the history of his anti-cop agenda. When publicly acknowledging his new role as the lead investigator and prosecutor, Ellison clearly contradicted any sense of "ordinary":[127]

> "This case is *unusual* because of the way that Mr. Floyd was killed and who did it; at the hands of the defendant who was a Minneapolis police officer..."

> "Let me also note *a dose of reality*... Prosecuting police officers for misconduct, including homicide and murder, is very difficult, and if you look at the cases that have been in front of the public in the last many years, it's easy to see that is true."

## Ellison and An Apparent Ethics Violation

Ellison glossed over the fact that Freeman convicted former Minneapolis Police Officer Mohamed Noor just the year before.[128] The bigger issue is that when Ellison offered his opinion about Derek Chauvin and the history of cases against police officers, Ellison apparently violated rules and ethics about media publicity. The Minnesota Rules of Professional Conduct codifies the things attorneys can and cannot say or do professionally. In making these

---

126. Minnesota Attorney General Keith Ellison to lead any prosecutions into George Floyd's death. (2020, June 1). *WCCO CBS Minnesota.*

127. Attorney General Keith Ellison to lead prosecution of George Floyd's death. (2020, May 31). *WCCO/CBS Minnesota*; emphasis added; Attorney General Keith Ellison. (n.d.) Prescription drug abuse is the fastest growing drug problem in the United States and in Minnesota. https://doseofreality.mn.gov/

128. Grinberg, E. (2019, May 1). Former Minneapolis police officer found guilty in Justine Ruszczyk's death. *CNN.*

remarks during a press conference, Ellison seems to have violated an important rule about trial publicity: [129]

> (RULE 3.6: TRIAL PUBLICITY)
> (a) A lawyer who is participating or has participated in the investigation or litigation of a criminal matter shall not make an extrajudicial statement about the matter that the lawyer knows or reasonably should know will be disseminated by means of public communication and will have a substantial likelihood of materially prejudicing a jury trial in a pending criminal matter.

According to the rule, a lawyer in Minnesota cannot make statements to the press or public that will unfairly influence a jury. Ellison was obviously speaking to the media, so he must have known his remarks about the *unusual* way that George Floyd was *killed* by "the hands of the defendant" could prejudice a jury trial. Ellison also made his prejudice about the case—and Chauvin's predetermined guilt—absolutely clear in another interview: [130]

> "I am committed to winning this case. That's what it's about for me. I would never charge everyone. Nor would I be part of a prosecution unless I believed the person was guilty and they needed to be held accountable."

In proving that he was obviously aware of the rules and ethics, when Ellison spoke to the media the next day, he carefully explained how the prosecution "won't be able to say much publicly as they build a case. They'll do their talking in court."[131] In demanding "justice for George Floyd" plenty of people were doing plenty of talking outside the courtroom before, during, and after

---

129. Minnesota rules of professional conduct. (2005, October 1). *Minnesota Legislature, Office of the Revisor of Statutes.*

130. Transcript: Into an American uprising: Keith Ellison on prosecuting George Floyd's death. (2020, June 2). *MSNBC.*

131. George Floyd death: All four ex-officers involved now charged, in custody. (2020, June 3). *WCCO.*

the trial. Some were also yelling, making violent threats, and letting Molotov cocktails do the talking.

## Maxine Waters and a Mistrial?

There are so many examples of political interference and attempts to unfairly influence the outcome of this case. However, US Representative Maxine Waters offered one of the best examples of how to basically cause a mistrial. Just three days before the jury announced a verdict, Waters—a democrat representing a district in California—was in Brooklyn Center, Minnesota. She spoke to a crowd protesting the police shooting of Duante Wright, which happened the week before. The remarks Waters shared with the crowd were hardly controversial. But what she told reporters afterward was nothing short of outrageous. When asked about the verdict she expected in the trial of Derek Chauvin, Waters seemed to send a warning:[132]

> "We're looking for a guilty verdict and we're looking to see if all of the talk that took place and has been taking place after they saw what happened to George Floyd. If nothing does not happen, then we know that we got to not only stay in the street, but we have got to fight for justice [...]"

> "We got to stay on the street. And we've got to get more active, we've got to get more confrontational. We've got to make sure that they know that we mean business."

For obvious reasons, Chauvin's defense attorney, Eric Nelson, requested a mistrial. He argued that impartiality didn't stand a chance against Waters' threats and inflammatory rhetoric:

---

132. Duster, C. (2021, April 19). Waters calls for protesters to 'get more confrontational' if no guilty verdict is reached in Derek Chauvin trial. *CNN*; Cillizza, C. (2021, April 19). Maxine Waters just inflamed a very volatile situation. *CNN*.

"I just don't know how this jury can really be said to be that they are free from the taint of this, and now that we have US representatives threatening acts of violence in relation to this specific case, it's—it's mind-boggling to me, Judge."

Judge Cahill agreed with Nelson and scolded politicians for interfering with the trial:

"I'm aware that Congresswoman Waters was talking specifically about this trial, and about the unacceptability of anything less than a murder conviction, and talk about being 'confrontational'...
I wish elected officials would stop talking about this case, especially in a manner that is disrespectful to the rule of law and to the judicial branch and our function... Their failure to do so, I think, is abhorrent..."

He also acknowledged the unreasonable influence of Water's remarks:

"[Waters] may have given you something on appeal that may result in this whole trial being overturned."

But what Judge Cahill said next was truly mind-boggling. After all his scorn, he summed up the whole matter by saying:[133]

"I don't think it's prejudiced us with additional material that would prejudice this jury [...] a congresswoman's opinion really doesn't matter a whole lot."

Judge Cahill denied the motion for a mistrial and allowed the case to proceed as if nothing happened—and as if the jury could ignore everything going on inside and outside the courtroom regarding the case.

---

133. Kelly, C. (2021, April 20). Judge in Derek Chauvin trial says Rep. Maxine Water's comments may be grounds for appeal. *CNN*.

## Remarks of an Attorney Are Not Evidence...

Judge Cahill also gave instructions about what was said *inside* the courtroom. He told the jury that "the arguments or other remarks of an attorney are not evidence" and should be ignored. That must have been challenging, especially since right after that, prosecutor Jerry Blackwell delivered his closing arguments. Although Blackwell didn't just use words; he also used symbolic images to persuade the jury. For example, Blackwell showed a photo of a bystander with a nine-year-old girl. They were standing on the sidewalk watching the police and George Floyd. The girl was wearing a shirt that said "Love."[134] After showing the photo, Blackwell then told the jury that George Floyd had a big heart—and that "the reason George Floyd is dead is because Mr. Chauvin's heart was too small." As *NPR* pointed out, Blackwell's comments would be "the last time the jury would hear from the lawyers" before deliberating their verdict."[135] Judge Cahill expected the jury to be impartial, but Blackwell's remarks certainly influenced the courtroom. Carolyn Pawlenty, Derek Chauvin's mother, told me that Blackwell's words had a profound affect upon her—but not in a positive way:[136]

> "Every day I heard so many lies, so many things that weren't true. But when I heard him say Derek had a small heart—I'm over 70 years old, I'm not a violent person—but I wanted to jump out of my chair when I heard that. When you hurt my son, you hurt me. I don't think any of those prosecutors understood that or cared about anyone else in the courtroom but themselves."

---

134. Forliti, A., Groves, S., & Webber, T. (2021, April 24). Key moments in closing arguments of Chauvin trial. *AP News*.

135. Kennedy, M., & Romo, V. (2021, April 19). Jurors have the case in Chauvin trial; Prosecutors ended with call for common sense. *NPR*.

136. C. Pawlenty (personal communication, September 4, 2022).

## What Prosecutors Didn't Say—And Didn't Want to be Heard

The prosecution obviously had a lot to say during the trial. However, what they *didn't say* also influenced the case. For example, prosecutors and witnesses talked about how George Floyd said he couldn't breathe. But they left out the part about *when* Floyd first said he had trouble breathing. Of course, the prosecution isn't going to do anything to jeopardize a conviction or create reasonable doubt. But attorneys supposedly have a duty to the court and to fairness. There's also the reality of the situation and the truth behind the circumstances, but those are often manipulated. As the bodycam videos of Lane and Kueng clearly show, Floyd seemed to have difficulty breathing *before* the squad car door was even opened.[137] While Floyd was resisting officers who were trying to get him inside the squad car, Floyd said:

> "I just had COVID, I don't want to go back to that."

> "When I start breathing, when I start breathing,
> it's gonna go off on me."

> "I'll get on the ground—anything."

> "I can't choke—I can't breathe, Mr. Officer."

It's not only what he was saying, but *when* he said it that matters. For the record, George Floyd said all of this *before* Derek Chauvin even touched him.

Also, when Charles McMillian, a bystander, noticed Floyd struggling with Officers Kueng and Lane, he told Floyd to stop "trying to win" and just get in the car. Floyd shouted back to McMillian:

> "I got anxiety. I don't want to do anything to them."

---

137. Body cam video of Officer Thomas Lane. [2020-05-25, 20:15: 40].

Floyd seemed to be saying that he didn't want to hurt Officers Kueng and Lane or was afraid he would lose control and do something to them. Words like that should raise a red flag for officer safety in any situation. Floyd also told officers, "I wanna lay on the ground, I wanna lay on the ground..." While Floyd continued to resist, McMillian seemed to have noticed that Floyd's physical condition was getting worse. McMillian told Floyd:[138]

"Get in the car! You're gonna have a heart attack."

In yelling back to McMillian, Floyd said: "I know, I can't breathe."

Derek Chauvin's knee was not on George Floyd's neck when he said this. Most people are unaware of these facts because none of this can be seen in the viral Facebook video. The video also doesn't show the number of times officers asked Floyd to sit inside the squad car—and how Floyd refused and ignored them every single time. All of this was recorded plain as day on the officers' body cameras, which might help to explain why the police body cam footage was kept from the public for so long.

## No Objections!

Obviously, the prosecution wanted to avoid everything Floyd said about not being able to breathe *before* Chauvin came in physical contact with him. One might think that the defense could show the police body cam videos and establish reasonable doubt. That's hardly a given, especially considering all of the objections and questionable rulings about the body cam footage and other evidence. This relates to another strange part of the jury instructions. Judge Cahill instructed the jury not to be concerned with objections to testimony and evidence:

---

138. Witness Charles McMillian says he told George Floyd 'you can't win' with police. (2021, March 31). *Fox 9 KMSP*.

"During this trial I have ruled on objections to certain testimony and exhibits. You must not concern yourself with the reasons for the rulings, since they are controlled by rules of evidence."

According to his instructions, every juror was supposed to ignore every "objection!" and other remarks about evidence and testimony throughout the trial. That's a bit unrealistic. However, telling jurors they shouldn't be concerned because the rulings are "controlled by rules of evidence" is just a smoke-and-mirrors way of sidestepping impartiality. Judge Cahill made every ruling about the evidence jurors could see and hear during the trial—and what they could not. That's what judges do. Some of the rulings might have seemed routine. But others were questionable, if not political. Obviously, denying the motion for a mistrial because of Maxine Waters' comments and interference would be one of the most significant decisions Judge Cahill made during the trial. Whether people believed Chauvin was guilty or not, everyone in America should be concerned about the compromises to impartiality in this case—and how the prosecution often seemed to be lying by omission.

## Lies—And Lying by Omission

Some of Judge Cahill's rulings influenced the outcome of this trial long before the jurors were even selected. One of the first decisions he made that set the course of the trial and influenced so many other aspects along the way, was a gag order issued on July 9, 2020. Judge Cahill might have been trying to prevent more outrage in trying to keep both the prosecution and the defense from talking to the media about the case. But it effectively allowed protesters and everybody else to label Chauvin a "murderer" and a "killer"—while barring the defense from saying a word in response.[139] Because of all the things the prosecution had already said to the media, Nelson filed an objection to the gag order on Chauvin's behalf, but it hardly changed the circumstances. The

---

139. Nelson, E. (2020, July 13). Defendant's objection to the court's *sua sponte* gag order. State of Minnesota v. Derek Chauvin, 27-CR-12646.

defense had no recourse other than to stay silent and standby as fairness disappeared with every accusation and every insult the media and the Left offered up about the "killing" of George Floyd.

## Hiding Police Body Cam Videos (The New Accountability)

The gag order also affected the handling of the police body cam videos. The rulings Judge Cahill made about the videos were some of the most bizarre decisions in the entire case. The rulings defied the handling of body cams in criminal trials in general. Long before the trial was underway, Judge Cahill ruled that body cam videos were not going to be released to the public. This was unheard of, as defense attorney Nelson explained:[140]

> "I've never seen that happen before. I've handled other cases that have had pretty intense media coverage. But the body cam videos were always released publicly."

This also went against the lessons that were learned the hard way in Minneapolis after the Jamar Clark incident on November 15, 2015. Clark was involved in a domestic assault. His female acquaintance was being treated for a broken ankle and other injuries when Clark began interfering with paramedics. When two MPD officers responded to help, Clark started fighting with them. The struggle quickly became violent, and Clark grabbed the gun of one of the officers. He was pulling the gun out of the officer's holster when the other officer shot Clark.[141] The officers were immediately accused of shooting an "unarmed Black man."[142] Clark may have been "unarmed." But he was trying to arm himself with an officer's gun. That didn't seem to matter much as

---

140. E. Nelson (personal communication, September 6, 2022).

141. Alsup, D., & Almasy, S. (2015, November 20). Lawyer: Jamar Clark had control of police officer's gun. *CNN;* Identity withheld (personal communication, October 10, 2022).

142. Chuck, E. (2015, November 19). Jamar Clark: Tension rises after killing of unarmed Minneapolis man. *NBC News.*

protesters and Black Lives Matter activists stoked outrage and "occupied" the area outside the MPD Fourth Precinct for 18 days.

Hennepin County Attorney Mike Freeman handled the case to determine whether the two officers who shot and killed Clark would face criminal charges. The officers were not charged. Subsequently, Freeman changed the way officer-involved shootings and in-custody deaths would be handled in the future. Instead of having grand juries decide, Freeman determined that his office would make the decisions about filing criminal charges against police officers. He believed that grand juries didn't provide transparency and accountability. During a public forum about the Clark case, Freeman said the "biggest regrets" in his career involved using grand juries and their lack of transparency in dealing with officer-involved homicides. Chief Harteau and Deputy Chief Arradondo were also there. So was Bob. He said, it's a "very bold move." But also questioned it—"what happens if an anti-police activist gets elected to county attorney? Does that mean that every officer involved in a shooting gets indicted?"[143]

Freeman claimed to be touting transparency in 2015. But there seems to be a difference between Freeman's principles and his practices. Despite demands from civil rights groups, BLM protesters who occupied the Fourth Precinct, and demonstrators throughout the city, Freeman and MPD leaders refused to release video footage from the Jamar Clark shooting. They claimed the BCA and the FBI were still investigating. If this sounds familiar, that's because it is. Police leaders and prosecutors were giving the public the run-around with the Jamar Clark case in 2015.

---

143. Chanen, D., & Jany, L. (2016, March 17). Hennepin County to stop using grand juries in officer-involved shootings. *Star Tribune*.

*Protesters at Minneapolis City Hall on December 3, 2015, demanding the release of video evidence related to the Jamar Clark shooting (Source: Fibonacci Blue, CC 2.0 licensing: https://creativecommons.org/licenses/by/2.0/)*

Five years later, they were doing the same thing with the George Floyd case. Freeman, who handled the Clark case, was also the initial prosecutor in Chauvin's case. He remained on the prosecution team when Attorney General Keith Ellison took over. Ellison, by the way, took on the role of community mediator during the unrest after the Jamar Clark shooting. In dealing with demands for video of the incident to be released, Ellison said, "I stood behind Black Lives Matter Minneapolis with these requests and have echoed them at every opportunity."[144]

---

144. Lopez, R. (2015, November 29). U.S. Rep. Ellison emerges as key political leader amid Jamar Clark protests. *Star Tribune;* I also interviewed Ellison and spoke with him during a press conference surrounded by protesters on November 19, 2015.

Now that Ellison was the attorney general of Minnesota, he didn't seem too eager to release the body cam videos in the George Floyd case. Granted, investigators need time to review police body cam footage to gather information without interference, especially since suspects, witnesses, and evidence tend to disappear once the public and the press find out about a case. Prosecutors may also have legitimate reasons for withholding footage— *initially.* Judges may need to do the same for the sake of impartiality and to avoid tainting the jury. But the George Floyd case was different. In fact, it seemed like the jury pool was already tainted not by what they would see, but what they *didn't* see. Millions of people have seen the viral Facebook video, but nobody was able to see the police body cam videos until months later. Allowing more police body cam video evidence in court might have helped provide some balance. When I asked Nelson if the jury was influenced more by what was omitted, and more by what they *didn't* see, he said, "Yeah, I think that's a rational conclusion."

It's difficult to imagine that any of this resembled fairness and impartiality. At the very least, keeping the police videos from the public and the press—along with Judge Cahill's gag order and his decisions and instructions about the body cam videos—allowed Ellison and the prosecution to maintain control of the narrative. It might seem obvious now: without the police videos, there was nothing to compare to the viral Facebook video. Since there was no basis for comparison, the viral Facebook video—and freeze-frame screenshots that were used extensively by the media and the Left—were etched into the collective memory of just about everyone in America.

Months later, when Judge Cahill allowed the body cam videos to be released, media access was extremely limited. His restrictions also challenged the right to a public trial and principles of the First Amendment. Judge Cahill's decisions seemed to obstruct transparency and accountability, much like Chief

Arradondo and Mayor Frey, who also refused to release the body cam footage. It appears they didn't learn anything from the riots in Ferguson, or the Jamar Clark incident, or the devastating riots that shattered Minneapolis.

## Behind the Scenes: What the Prosecution Was Really Doing

The evidence withheld or ruled out in this case had a much greater influence upon the trial than most people probably realize. On May 26, 2020, Minneapolis was on the brink of chaos. Releasing the videos could have helped to quell the outrage, if not prevent it in the first place. But from the moment Arradondo told Bob that he called in the FBI, it seems county attorneys were far more interested in building a case than keeping the peace. While the videos were being kept from the public and the police union, prosecutors were planning to share them with an "expert" witness. They were also planning to share other evidence, including surveillance videos, memos about Dr. Baker's initial autopsy findings, and MPD policies. This all started the day after George Floyd was arrested and died. The prosecution spent days making arrangements, but that wasn't documented in a memo until nearly two weeks later. This wasn't the only memo with odd dates. When the defense filed a motion to disqualify, they included another peculiar memo from the prosecution. It was written by county attorney Patrick Lofton and dated May 26, 2020. But somehow it referred to a meeting in the future that had yet to occur on May 27th. This could have been a simple oversight. But since the meeting likely shouldn't have happened in the first place, the strange dates seemed even more suspicious.

```
┌─────────────────────────────────────────┐
│    HENNEPIN COUNTY ATTORNEY'S OFFICE      │
│        Adult Prosecution Division         │
│          M E M O R A N D U M              │
└─────────────────────────────────────────┘
```

**TO:**  File

**FROM:** Amy Sweasy and Patrick Lofton

**RE:**  George Floyd – UDF Case

**DATE:** June 11, 2020

On Tuesday, May 26th, Amy Sweasy (AS) texted Chief Tim Longo (TL) of the University of Virginia (UVA) Police Department. TL was our expert in the *Noor* case. Last fall, TL went back into full time police work as the chief for UVA PD and was no longer taking on new cases as a police practices expert. AS did not hear back from TL that day and texted him again on the morning of Wednesday, May 27th.

On the evening of the 27th, AS and Patrick Lofton (PL) were in AS's office watching BWC video and AS got a text from an unknown number saying it was TL and he was wondering about the situation in Mpls. We called TL right away and he said he had a new cell phone number that we didn't have. We discussed what little we knew at that point and asked TL if he would work with us as a police practices expert. He said he needed to get permission from his employer, UVA, and he would let us know the next day. We began to make arrangements for TL to get BWC video and other materials by FedEx.

On May 28, Angela Erichson sent TL a USB drive via FedEx containing:
1. Kueng BWC
2. Lane BWC
3. Cup Foods surveillance video
4. Street camera surveillance video
5. Memo re: Dr. Baker 5-26-2020
6. Memo re: Dr. Baker 5-27-2020
7. MPD Critical Incident Policy (51 pages)
8. MPD Policy and Procedure Manual (542 pages).

Later that night from an offsite location, Ms. Erichson worked with Hennepin County Attorney IT to send Kueng and Lane BWC via a secure cloud link to TL so that he could watch them on the night of the 28th and not wait for FedEx.

TL agreed to serve as an expert for us on this case. He sent a retainer agreement to us by email which was never executed.

*Memo dated June 11, 2020, from county prosecutor Amy Sweasy (AS) detailing plans to share the body worn camera (BWC) footage with an expert witness, Chief Tim Longo (TL) on May 26. Motion to disqualify. State of Minnesota v. Derek Chauvin, 27-CR-20-12646 (August 28, 2020).*

---

**HENNEPIN COUNTY ATTORNEY'S OFFICE**
**Adult Prosecution Division**
**M E M O R A N D U M**

---

TO:      File

FROM:   Patrick Lofton

RE:      George Floyd – UDF Case
             Meeting with Medical Examiner

DATE:   May 26, 2020

---

On May 27, 2020, Patrick Lofton, Amy Sweasy, Mike Freeman, and Andrew LeFevour met with Hennepin County Medical Examiner Dr. Andrew Baker in person in a socially distanced room.

Dr. Baker provided the same autopsy presentation from the May 26, 2020 Microsoft Teams Meeting, as well as the following additional information:

Some of the scars on Mr. Floyd's hand were preexisting and likely from an incident in which he broke some glass and was admitted to the hospital approximately a month prior.

AB recalled there were indications in Mr. Floyd's medical records that he had been admitted to methamphetamine detox.

AB reiterated that his findings are preliminary and that he has not issued a final report. He opined the ultimate cause of death may prove to be a multifactorial diagnosis. Based on what AB knows so far, the three factors in that diagnosis could be (1) coronary artery disease, (2) any stimulants potentially in Mr. Floyd's system causing his heart to work harder, and (3) the exertion caused by Mr. Floyd's encounter with the police officers. This would depend on the quality and intensity of the encounter.

In AB's experience, overexertion of the heart is one of the reason police departments avoid using the type of hold at issue. AB still had not seen any videos.

022942

---

*A memo from the Hennepin County Attorney's Office dated May 26, 2020—describing a meeting that occurred the day after. Motion to disqualify. State of Minnesota v. Derek Chauvin, 27-CR-20-12646 (August 28, 2020).*

## George Floyd Sold Opioids During an Undercover Sting

Aside from questionable dates, one of the memos from the prosecution indicated that George Floyd "had been admitted to methamphetamine detox." This was just part of the evidence about Floyd's history of drug abuse and violent crime that was mostly withheld from the jury. Judge Cahill made decisions to withhold the body cameras. He also made decisions that limited evidence about Floyd's past drug abuse, including how he was arrested for selling more than 1,000 illegal oxycodone pills during an undercover narcotics investigation. How Floyd was able to get so many pills is another story.

Judge Cahill gave instructions to the jury about how they were supposed to handle and *ignore* parts of this evidence. His instructions were titled "Evidence of Other Occurrences Involving George Floyd." It might sound like something from a nineteenth-century detective novel. But it was about how the jury was supposed to only use the evidence to evaluate what happened after Floyd swallowed pills during his arrest in 2019 and was apparently trying to destroy evidence. Judge Cahill instructed the jury accordingly:

> "You have heard evidence of an occurrence involving George Floyd on May 6, 2019. As I told you at the time this evidence was offered, it was admitted solely for the limited purpose of showing what effects the ingestion of opioids may or may not have had on the physical wellbeing of George Floyd."

The judge wanted the jury to focus on Floyd's "wellbeing." This greatly limited the ability of Chauvin's defense attorney to use or question the evidence for any other purpose. Obviously, this posed significant problems for the defense, especially since it could have helped to establish a clear pattern of criminal behavior. George Floyd swallowed pills when he was arrested in 2019—and he did the same when he was arrested by Chauvin and the other officers in 2020. The body cam videos from George Floyd's arrest in 2019 and his arrest in 2020 show many of the same odd behaviors. During both arrests,

Floyd was resisting commands from police officers. He refused to get out of the car. He appeared to swallow pills. He was also acting erratic, crying, and asking for his "momma." However, the jury had to follow Judge Cahill's instructions and focus on his "wellbeing" and ignore everything else.

Of course, pointing out George Floyd's criminal behavior would undermine the prosecution's attempt to prove Chauvin guilty. Ellison was determined to win a conviction and was already convinced that Chauvin was guilty and needed to be held accountable. But Ellison and the prosecution still had to "prove" it in court.[145] So, of course the prosecution tried to exclude the 2019 arrest. The media and the left were doing their part claiming that any evidence of Floyd's prior arrests or criminal history was nothing but an attempt to "smear Mr. Floyd's character by showing what he struggled with, an opioid addiction like so many Americans do."[146] On the other hand, excluding evidence from the 2019 arrest could have helped Chauvin win an appeal or establish grounds for a mistrial. In what seems like an attempt to reckon the situation, Judge Cahill made the decision to allow *some* of the evidence from the 2019 arrest, but he drastically limited the purpose and scope of it.

### A Different Dose of Reality?

If this case happened to be about facts and evidence—as an impartial trial should be—then such drastic decisions and strange instructions about the scope of evidence shouldn't have been necessary. But protesters and activists were adamant that George Floyd's character should not be put on trial, or even

---

145. Transcript: Into an American uprising: Keith Ellison on prosecuting George Floyd's death. (2020, June 2). *MSNBC*.

146. McEvoy, J. (2021, April 13). Chauvin defense opens case by highlighting a previous arrest of George Floyd. *Forbes*.

questioned for that matter. In offering his closing arguments, prosecutor Steve Schleicher adamantly explained:[147]

> "We need to be clear—this is not the trial of George Floyd. George Floyd is not on trial here."

So, with that in mind, it seems Judge Cahill's decisions about evidence might have been attempts to avoid the "optics" of showing Floyd's criminal behavior. Allowing more evidence would have indicated a pattern of criminal behavior. It also could've revealed how Floyd may have contributed or caused his own death by swallowing pills. The pills he swallowed in 2019 were likely just opioids, based on the ones he sold and the ones he still had. But the pills he apparently swallowed in 2020 contained fentanyl (an opioid) and methamphetamine (a stimulant): a dangerous and even fatal combination known as a "speedball."[148]

Allowing more of this evidence could have easily made the proceedings look like "the trial of George Floyd," as Schleicher affirmed was not supposed to be the case. It also could have undermined the prosecution's ability to prove the murder charges against Chauvin beyond a reasonable doubt. The fact that Floyd was addicted to opioids looked bad enough for the prosecution.[149] Beyond the optics, allowing evidence indicating that Floyd might have caused his own death would have made Ellison look bad in more ways than one.

---

147. Casiano, L., & Wallace, D. (2021, April 19). Derek Chauvin closing arguments end, jurors to begin deliberation. *Fox News.*

148. Pichini, S., Solimini, R., Berretta, P., Pacifici, R., & Busardò, F. (2018). Acute intoxications and fatalities from illicit fentanyl and analogues: An update. *Therapeutic Drug Monitoring, 40*(1), 38-51.

149. Girlfriend of George Floyd speaks about their drug use: "Classic story of how many people get addicted." (2021, April 1). *MSNBC.*

As Minnesota's attorney general, Ellison promised to "crack down on the opioid epidemic."[150] As part of that effort, he promoted the "Dose of Reality" anti-opioid abuse campaign. The campaign warned that:[151]

> "Taking just one dose too large can cause serious health problems and potentially lead to death.
>
> ...the risk of overdose and death increases exponentially when prescription painkillers are combined with other drugs or alcohol."

According to the autopsy, that is, both the official autopsy report and the review by the Office of The Armed Forces Medical Examiner, George Floyd had both fentanyl and methamphetamine in his system. This was precisely the combination of opioids and other drugs that Ellison's campaign warned about. While Ellison was boldly crusading against opioid abuse in public, his prosecution team was trying to downplay George Floyd's opioid addiction and drug dealing during Chauvin's trial. Obviously, this suggests a lot more was going on behind the scenes than the jurors and the public may have realized.

Chauvin and Eric Nelson, his defense attorney, were certainly baffled by Judge Cahill's rulings about evidence and testimony during the trial. Some of the witnesses for the defense also wondered what was going on, including Officer Scott Creighton. Creighton was injured during the riots in 2020, and arrested George Floyd the year before. At first, Creighton was subpoenaed to testify for the prosecution. But he ended up testifying for the defense and was called as their first witness. His body cam video of Floyd's arrest on May 6, 2019, was

---

150. Priorities, Keith Ellison for Minnesota Attorney General. (n.d.). https://www.keithellison.org/priorities.

151. Attorney General Keith Ellison. (n.d.). Prescription drug abuse is the fastest growing drug problem in the United States and in Minnesota. https://doseofreality.mn.gov/

submitted as evidence and played in court.[152] The video was more than 20 minutes long, but only about a minute of it admitted was shown to the jury due to objections and Judge Cahill's rulings. The story about how this came about reveals some of the politics at play, which apparently gave the prosecution an unfair advantage. It also reveals how jurors did not see key evidence about George Floyd's criminal behavior and drug dealing.

### Interview with Scott Creighton (Part II)

"I can't go into all the details and say where this happened, but we had it all set up early that morning [May 6, 2019]. The narcotics guys set up a rip—that's a drug deal set up through an informant, and when the dealer drives up, you stop the car, and make the arrest. They ordered 1,000 pills of oxycodone. But this time, we didn't hit it right away, we waited, and let the buy go down. We took down the car after the money was exchanged. I think they ended up getting over a thousand pills. I was in the take-down squad at the time. We were the first to pull over the vehicle. I went up to the passenger side—and I can't really explain it better than my body cam video—but I go up to the passenger side and there's Floyd. If you look at the video, it's the same whole scenario, the same behaviors, almost everything goes the same way like it did for Chauvin and those guys. All that stuff Floyd was saying about his "momma" and all of that, it was all very similar. I don't know if I was lucky, but it worked out, even after Floyd put something in his mouth and was resisting the whole time."

"Once we got to the precinct, I had to walk him downstairs. Like the video shows, he's not having any problem. He's talking to me normally. When we get him down to the interview room, that's when he starts talking about how he needs medical, or an ambulance, or this and that. But then he starts saying,

---

152. Exhibit 1051. State of Minnesota v. Derek Chauvin, 27-CR-20-12646. The video was published in October 2020 on behalf of former officer Thomas Lane.

"I feel faint." Whenever somebody says something like that, we immediately call for an ambulance. You don't want to be responsible if something happens because you're going to be taking the fall for it."

"The paramedics came right down to our interview room—by the way, this is something that didn't come out in the trial—when they checked him out, Floyd's blood pressure was like four times as high as a normal person. They were going to take him to North (North Memorial Medical Center). Then when he gets upstairs, he decides he didn't want to go. They had to release him from their custody or put a medical hold on him. I was just there for the arrest, so I don't know what happened after that. I left when medical was still trying to figure out what to do with him."

"As for the charges we had on him, well, once again, he wasn't showing his hands because he was hiding stuff. Along with what he delivered, we found a bunch of pills right there underneath him, where he was sitting in the car. He was swallowing them and stuffing them when he wasn't showing me *his hands*. At first, I couldn't tell what he was doing. I didn't know if he had a gun, I couldn't see exactly. But I mean, we just set up a rip, and like five out of ten times, somebody has a gun. So, when someone's not putting their hands up, they're either tucking dope or a gun or doing something. That's why I acted the way I did."

"And here's something else that didn't come out during the trial. I don't know what exactly happened to the case after he was arrested in 2019. Last I heard, they deferred it or the county attorney denied it. Whatever happened, we never went to trial on that case. But it was Floyd who sold the pills and made the deal."

"With the Chauvin trial, at first I was subpoenaed by the prosecution. They knew I arrested George Floyd. They wanted to know everything I had to say about his behavior and the previous arrest. So, I went in for the pre-trial meeting. I get escorted upstairs into a meeting room, and we start reviewing the video and all that. But then Ellison, walks in. I thought to myself, why is Ellison here? At the time, I didn't know the case was being prosecuted by the Attorney General's office."

"Ellison gets some coffee and grabs a donut. Then he puts his chair back and puts his feet up and starts giving me the stink eye. I mean, I know him. I've dealt with him since he was a defense attorney when I was doing narc cases. But he's staring at me like I'm a dirty cop. I'm here as a witness *for the prosecution*—so I'm wondering why the Attorney General is looking at me like I'm guilty, like I did something wrong? He was looking at me the whole time, not just with disdain—it was more than disdain—and I'm a prosecution witness. While we're reviewing the video, I notice Ellison is going through my file to see if I had anything bad in there, which of course, I didn't. But that's when I figured out what he was doing."

"At that time, another prosecutor walked in, the one who did most of the prosecuting during the trial [Steve Schleicher]. He sat down with Ellison and they started asking me general questions, this and that. But then he asked what kind of a stop this was. I told him it was part of a narcotics investigation. He said, 'Don't you mean a traffic stop?' I said, no, it wasn't a traffic stop. I told him look at my report, right at the very beginning, it says we conducted a felony stop after a drug deal. Then both of them, Ellison and the prosecutor, asked me a few more times, 'Don't you mean a traffic stop?'—as if I didn't answer them already. So, after the third or fourth time, I explained that we already had probable cause for a felony stop because of the drug deal. Floyd was under arrest the moment we stopped him. I was sitting there wondering what is going on, they knew exactly what happened. It was right there in my report, right in front of them. They were reading from it. I couldn't believe it, but they asked me the same thing again. At this point, it felt like they weren't asking me questions for an answer. They were trying to get me to lie about what I wrote. So, I got adamant. I said, look, it's right there, 'stop and arrest.' It was a felony stop after a drug deal, and—"

"The prosecutor stood up and walked away before I could even finish what I was saying. Ellison called over some other guy and the three of them talked in secret for a minute or two. Then the prosecutor came back over to me and said, 'You're done. We don't need you, you're dismissed' or something like that. I was like what the heck is going on here? I mean, whenever you get called into court, the prosecutors go over every bit of your testimony. They ask all kinds of questions and go over everything. But they stopped right there. Then I get a call from Chauvin's attorney. He tells me the prosecution isn't going to call me as a witness. But he said that he would, for the defense, for Chauvin. So, that's how I went from being a witness for the prosecution to being a witness for Chauvin. But that was good. I didn't want to be a witness for the prosecution. As a cop, you've got to do what you've got to do and what the prosecution asks. But this case was different. With all that was going on, I thought I needed an attorney for myself. I didn't get one, but I was nervous about testifying. It didn't matter which side I was on because look at what they were doing to people. I knew the prosecution, the media—they were going to take my testimony and twist it around one way or another. That's what they were doing when they kept asking about when we arrested Floyd, and the nonsense about the traffic stop."

"I was worried about what was going to happen. I'm a cop, but I had to contact the sheriff's office and tell them I was witness for Derek Chauvin. I told them they were terrorizing my union president for nothing. So, I didn't know what might happen, if they'd shoot up my house or set it on fire—and that was before the trial even started. I was really worried after they did all of that stuff with the pig's head and smearing blood all over the house of the guy who testified after me.[153] My family was worried, too. My daughter was still in high school, so she was completely freaked out. That whole situation... I don't know... it was not good. I also knew they were going to come after my testimony.

That's why I went over everything again and again. I wanted to be clear on the facts. But I also didn't want to use any language that would incite anything or make them come after me. So, I took notes about the questions they were going to ask and what to say, and that's what I testified about. And just like I thought, my words were right there in the national news. I'm not the smartest guy on the planet. But when it comes to being streetwise and protecting yourself, I'm not the dumbest either. When I got home that night, on TV, and then in the newspaper the next day, the same things in my notes and what I said on the stand were right there. Here are the notes I quickly wrote out that I had on the stand. When I got the paper the next day, that's what was right below my picture..."

---

153. Creighton was referring to witness Barry Brodd. Three suspects were arrested and released: Rowan Dalbey, Kristen Aumoithe, and Amber Lucas. The suspects bragged about the crime on social media, while the media and the Left tried to downplay it. See Vera, A. (2021, April 19). Pig's blood was smeared on the former home of the use-of-force expert who testified for the defense in Chauvin's trial, police say. *CNN.*

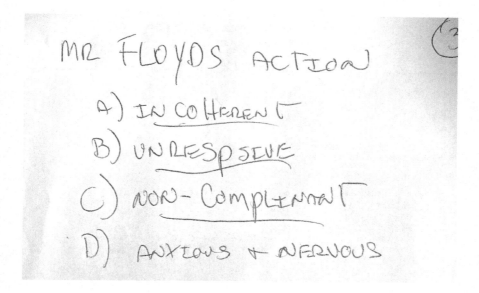

*Part of the notes Scott Creighton wrote and used while testifying during the trial of Derek Chauvin on April 13, 2021 (Courtesy of Scott Creighton, photo by Dr. JC Chaix).*

*A photo of the Star Tribune newspaper Scott Creighton bought quoting his testimony and his notes (Photo by Dr. JC Chaix).*

**MINNEAPOLIS POLICE DEPARTMENT**

**GENERAL OFFENSE HARDCOPY**

Incident Date 05/06/2019

(NARCOTICS VIOLATION)

GO# MP 2019-127538

NOT APPROVED

## Narrative Text Page(s)

### Narrative Text

**Type** NON-PUBLIC NARRATIVE

**Subject**

**Author** 1331 - CREIGHTON, SCOTT

**Related Date** May-06-2019 15:09

On 5/6/2019, at approximately 1150 hours, I was working Marked Squad 481, P#76678, with Officer ▇▇▇▇ we were both wearing BWC's.

We were contacted by Officer ▇▇▇ in regards to a 'Narcotics Investigation he was conducting. He informed us that a vehicle would be arriving in the area of ▇▇▇▇▇▇▇▇▇▇ Ave No., with a large amount of Oxycodin pills.

At approximately 1155 hours, we were informed to stop and arrest all parties inside a Maroon Ford Explorer, with unlicensed plates. We drove into the area and observed the Maroon Ford Explore without plates drivng E/B on ▇▇▇▇▇▇▇▇▇▇ Ave No. We then activated the overhead lights and made a traffic stop on the vehicle. The vehicle turned N/B on ▇▇▇▇▇ No., and the vehicle stopped. There were (2) parties in the vehicle, the driver/AP Hicks and the passenger/AP Floyd.

We approached the vehicle, ordered them to turn the vehicle off and then exit the vehicle. The driver/AP Hicks was removed first. I then approached on the passenger side of the vehicle and met with passenger/AP Floyd. AP Floyd was moving all around and acting extremely nervous and would not listen to my commands. I continued to order him several times to stop moving around and to see his hands. AP Floyd had also put something in his mouth and was attempting to eat them. He was informed to spit what he had in his mouth out, but had already ate them.

Officer ▇▇▇▇ and myself then had to physically remove AP Floyd from the vehicle and then handcuff him. AP Floyd continue to talk and then began to cry. I conducted a pat-down search and during the search, I felt a budge in his stomach area and removed a white napkin. The napkin contained several pills of Oxycodin. AP Floyd also had cash in both his front pockets. I removed and recovered the cash. The cash amount was $594.00. AP Floyd was walked over to the squad, while walking him to the squad, (2) Oxycodon pills fell out of his pant leg to the ground. The pills were recovered and put with the other pills found on AP Floyd.

After AP Floyd was placed in the rear of the squad, I then went back up to the passenger side of the vehicle and in plain view could see several Oxycodin pills on passenger seat. I observed a brown pouch on the passenger floor board and picked it up and opened it. Inside the brown pouch was found several packages of pills and powder cocaine. I also found paperwork with the name of AP

*A copy of Officer Scott Creighton's narrative about the arrest of George Floyd on May 6, 2019.*
*AP is an abbreviation for "Arrested Person" (Obtained and redacted by Dr. JC Chaix).*

"The last thing I wanted to say was this, for whatever reason Chauvin's defense attorney didn't want to push the felony traffic stop either. I don't know what the angle was, but nobody said it was a felony stop. Nobody did, and I wasn't going to correct them. So, I don't know if the judge made a ruling, but there had to be something that kept my testimony that limited."

"What they left out—and what nobody mentioned during the trial—was the reason why we stopped Floyd, which was the drug deal. The other guy wasn't our suspect, Floyd was. Floyd delivered the pills. We found the money in his pocket. I photographed and recovered all of that. For whatever reason, all that was excluded during Chauvin's trial. There was something like 22 minutes of video of me arresting Floyd. But they limited that down to like a minute and only three questions. I don't know how trial attorney stuff works, but there were a lot more questions they were going to ask. So, whether it was Ellison or the judge, they limited the scope almost down to nothing. But whatever they were trying to do with the jury, the truth is still out there. If you look at the videos from the arrest of Floyd, and my video from 2019, and compare them side by side, I mean they're almost identical."

## Swallowing Evidence or Chewing Gum?

When Creighton took the stand, Judge Cahill gave instructions to the jury about the strict purpose of the evidence. After testifying for the defense, Creighton was cross-examined by prosecutor Erin Eldridge—just another one of the many prosecutors involved in the trial. Eldridge appeared annoyed and agitated when she sharply asked Creighton for clarifications. Then she asked what seemed like the most inflammatory, insensitive, and *completely unnecessary* question during the whole trial:

> "Mr. Floyd didn't *drop dead* while you were interacting with him, correct?"

Creighton simply responded, "No."

It was a strange cross-examination to say the least.[154] Eldridge was apparently trying to prove that even though Floyd swallowed pills, his "well-being" wasn't affected. Floyd's arrest in 2019 obviously had a different outcome than his arrest in 2020. The pills were also apparently different as well. Creighton and the other narcotics officers recovered opioid pills (without methamphetamine) in 2019. But in 2020, as indicated by the autopsy report, Floyd had fentanyl and methamphetamine in his system. Nelson later called McKenzie Anderson to the witness stand. Anderson, a forensics scientist with the BCA, testified that George Floyd's DNA was found on chewed-up pills she recovered from the back of Chauvin's police car. The pills contained fentanyl and methamphetamine, like the pills found inside the car where Floyd was sitting.[155] As seen on the bodycam videos from Officer Lane and Officer Kueng, Floyd says, "I was hooping earlier," which is slang for doing drugs.

---

154. Collins, J., Williams, B., Sepic, M., & Feshir, R. (2021, April 13). Chauvin trial: Ex-cop did not use deadly force on Floyd, expert testifies. *MPR News*.

155. Fitz-Gibbon, G. (2021, April 7). Derek Chauvin lawyers discovered George Floyd 'speedball' in squad car. *New York Post*.

*A screenshot from Thomas Lane's body cam showing George Floyd with something in his mouth. Motion to dismiss. State of Minnesota v. Derek Chauvin, 27-CR-20-12646 (August 28, 2020).*

## Morries Hall, George Floyd's Drug Dealer

There's probably a lot of truth to that. Floyd was sitting in a car with his friend and drug dealer, Morries Hall.[156] Officer Lane explained what happened after he approached the car that Floyd, Hall, and Shawanda Hill were sitting in. Lane said, "[Hall] gave me a fake ID. So, in addition to the counterfeit $20 bill, he had drugs on him, and a felony warrant for his arrest."[157] Lane also explained that somehow Hall was released at the scene. As Lane learned through his own trial, Hall said that Floyd was unconscious for about a minute and a half. But he woke up just before Lane knocked on the window. Lane said the prosecution didn't want Hall to testify, and given the situation, Hall didn't

---

156. Zhao, C. (2021, May 4). Derek Chauvin judge unfairly blocked evidence from drug dealer Morries Hall, motion, says. *Newsweek*; Gockowski, A. (2021, April 1). George Floyd's friend, alleged drug dealer pleads the fifth. *Alpha News*.

157. T. Lane (personal communication, July 1, 2022).

want to testify either. So, Hall pleaded the fifth. Lane said there was a lot more to the story. For example, that Hall threw a baggie down in the street that day, or that he tried to leave town and take a Greyhound bus to Texas. Lane said the most frustrating part was that Hall was never charged with any of this, the fake ID, the counterfeit bills, or the drugs.

### "I Ate Too Many Drugs…"

The jury never heard about this or Hall's testimony because he plead the fifth. However, there was something defense attorney Nelson wanted the jury to hear and understand. It was something Floyd said himself. As Nelson pointed out, Floyd said that he was "hooping" and minutes later seemed to yell out, "I ate too many drugs." Nelson asked another witness, BCA Special Agent James Reyerson, about what Floyd said. After showing the video, Nelson asked:

"Did it appear that Mr. Floyd said, 'I ate too many drugs'?"

Special Agent Reyerson affirmed, "Yes it did."

When Reyerson was questioned by the prosecution, he changed his testimony and said, "I believe Mr. Floyd was saying, 'I ain't do no drugs'."[158] Even though there was video evidence of Floyd with something in his mouth, and his DNA was on chewed-up pills, and evidence that Floyd made a slang reference to doing drugs and possibly another about eating drugs, the prosecution dismissed it all: Floyd was just chewing gum. Due to Judge Cahill's decision about evidence and his instructions to the jury, the defense couldn't do more to show a pattern of Floyd's criminal behavior to counter the prosecution and demonstrate reasonable doubt.

---

158. Bosman, J. (2021, April 7). In the Chauvin trial, an argument emerges over whether George Floyd said he 'ate too many drugs' or 'ain't do no drugs.' *The New York Times*.

## "I Got Shot Last Time"

However, there are more than a few reasons to doubt that Floyd was just sitting in a car chewing gum. There are also plenty of reasons to doubt a lot of what he said. When Officer Lane initially approached George Floyd, Floyd was ignoring his commands (as he did when Officer Creighton approached him the year before). After Floyd kept refusing Lane's commands, Lane drew his gun. Floyd began to comply somewhat. Then Floyd explained, "I got shot last time, same thing." Floyd was apparently lying. If Floyd meant the "last time" he was arrested, that probably would have been with Officer Creighton in 2019. Creighton's body cam video clearly shows that he did not shoot Floyd. There's also no mention of anyone named George Floyd in *The Washington Post* police shooting database, which has been tracking police shootings since 2015. But perhaps the most telling thing about how Floyd seemed to be lying is that the media and the Left have ignored what he said. There aren't any news articles that explain whether he was actually shot or lying about it. Even more telling, the autopsy report didn't mention any gunshot wounds either.

Shawanda Hill, who was in the car when officers Lane and Kueng approached, seemed to go along with Floyd's claim. Hill was sitting in the backseat, and yelled, "Stop resisting Floyd!" when he refused to follow police commands.[159] When Officer Lane asked her why Floyd was acting weird, she said, "because he's been shot before." When Officer Lane asked her if Floyd was drunk or on drugs, she explained,

> "No... he got a thing going on, I'm telling you, about the police ... He have problems all the time when they come, especially when that man put that gun like that."

---

159. This was recorded on Officer Lane's body camera video, but it was not included in a transcription; cf. Exhibit 4. State of Minnesota v. Thomas Lane, 27-CR-20-12951; and Thomas Lane's body cam video, 2020-05-25 20:11:08 (Axon Body 3 X6039A5Z7); Thomas Lane bodycam video of George Floyd death. (2020, August 10). *Fox 9 KMSP*.

**George Floyd Was Arrested for Aggravated Robbery with a Firearm**

Whatever she meant by "thing going on" isn't exactly clear. Although given Floyd's violent criminal history, he has used guns against other people. In 2009, Floyd pled guilty to aggravated robbery with a deadly weapon. One of his accomplices, disguised himself as a water department worker and forced his way into a home in 2007. Floyd and four other suspects then went inside and confronted two women. A one-year-old child was with them. Floyd held a gun to a pregnant woman's stomach while the other suspects searched for money and drugs. Floyd then searched for himself, while another suspect held the woman at gunpoint and pistol-whipped her when she screamed for help. Floyd was sentenced to five years in prison.[160]

**Floyd Was Arrested for Cocaine Possession, and Theft with a Firearm**

Prior to that incident, Floyd was arrested and sentenced three times for cocaine possession:

> In December 2005, Floyd was sentenced to 10 months in jail.

> In 2004, he was sentenced to 10 months.

> In October 2002, he was sentenced to eight months. He was also arrested for criminal trespassing and sentenced to 30 days.

> In 1998, Floyd was sentenced to 10 months for theft with a firearm.

There was obviously more to the story about Floyd being shot and how he used guns against other people. However, there was something he apparently lied about that was even more significant—and it might have saved his life if he told the truth instead.

---

160. State of Texas v. George Floyd, Case No. 1143230, Incident No./TRN 9162821113A001, (April 3, 2009).

Officer Lane asked Floyd if he took drugs: "Are you on something right now?"

Floyd said: "—No, nothing."[161]

## Ellison: Keeping the Status Quo

It's difficult to think about how the situation could have been different if Floyd told the truth. Likewise, it seems Ellison and his prosecution team were doing more than just presenting facts. They were apparently discounting evidence and lying by omission to win a conviction. Which seems strange because Ellison was once eager to play the role of peacemaker and mediator during the unrest following the Jamar Clark shooting. But now that he was on the other side of the courtroom, Ellison seemed to be weaponizing the role of the prosecution within the criminal justice system—precisely one of the things protesters and reformers have been fighting against. Ellison once stood up for BLM and their demands for releasing the police body cam footage. But now he seemed to be preventing the release of the footage. This doesn't seem much different from how Ellison has handled other cases in the past, particularly the ones involving his allies and associates. On more than one occasion, Attorney General Ellison apparently weighed in on cases that were suddenly found to have "weak" charges or "insufficient evidence." For example, in 2019, MPD had a warrant to search the residence where ex-convict Samuel "Sharif" Willis was staying. Despite having discovered evidence of a crime, Sharif was released almost immediately after he was arrested, and the case against him was soon dismissed. To understand how or why this happened requires a brief look at Ellison's past, long before his involvement in the Jamar Clark case and the Derek Chauvin trial.

---

161. Thomas Lane bodycam video of George Floyd death. (2020, August 10). *Fox 9 KMSP*.

For those unfamiliar with Minneapolis crime history, Sharif Willis is a former high-ranking member of the Vice Lords gang. After serving decades in prison for weapons and drug charges, he supposedly turned his life around. He founded an organization called United for Peace along with local church pastor Jerry McAfee. Their vision was to stop the gang violence that was raging out of control in Minneapolis during the late 1980s and '90s. It was one of those stories of redemption we love to believe: a young gang member goes to prison, turns his life around, and helps others avoid the same fate.

### The Murder of Officer Jerry Haaf
That changed when Minneapolis police officer Jerry Haaf was shot and killed. On September 25, 1992, around two in the morning, Officer Haaf was taking a break at the Pizza Shack, a well-known local cop hangout. Haaf was drinking a cup of coffee and reading the newspaper when two Vice Lord gang members came in from behind and shot and executed him. Officer Haaf died about two hours later at the hospital.

Sharif was supposed to be a reformed gang leader doing his part to prevent violence in the community. However, his own nephew Monterey Willis, was suspected of helping to plan the execution. He also drove one of the getaway cars and helped provide the guns and ammo that were used in slaying Officer Haaf. Monterey was one of four suspects; the other three were A.C. Ford Jr. (aka Adl El-Shabazz); Shannon Bowles (aka Nantambu Kambon); and Mwati "Pepi" McKenzie. A few days after Officer Haaf was shot and killed, three of the suspects were located at Curly's Cafe. Squad cars swarmed the front, while Bob and his partner apprehended Monterey as he tried to run out of the back. While they were bringing Monterey in for questioning, he kept taunting Bob and his partner, saying things like, "You know you want to kill me, you know you want to... why don't you just do it?"

## Officer Haaf's Killer Arrested at Sharif Willis' House

That night, investigators didn't have enough evidence, so the suspects were questioned and released. But not long afterward, Monterey was arrested along with Bowles—in the driveway at Sharif's house. The two were about to skip town when they were caught. According to court documents:[162]

> "[they] had been involved in the killing and were preparing to flee to Texas in a black Cadillac or a Chevrolet Beretta. [...]
>
> That evening, at about 9:30 p.m., police went to Sharif Willis' home. They found the Cadillac packed with clothing and arrested both Bowles and appellant (Monterey Willis)."

Pepi McKenzie, one of the other suspects, had already skipped town for Chicago. He was soon brought back to Minneapolis and surrendered to police. McKenzie was accompanied by Vice Lords gang leader Farley Cotton, Pastor McAfee, a KARE 11 TV reporter and cameraman—and then-attorney Keith Ellison. KARE 11 chartered a plane to bring McKenzie from Chicago back to Minneapolis.[163] Ultimately, all four suspects were convicted for their involvement in the execution of Officer Haaf. By the way, the prosecutor in this case was Mike Freeman, the same prosecutor working with Ellison in prosecuting Chauvin.

During the trials for the murder of Officer Haaf, two people testified about Sharif's involvement in Haaf's murder. As court records indicated:

> "A.C. Ford, who was second in command of the [Vice Lords] gang, proposed the idea of shooting a police officer at the Pizza Shack during a meeting at the home of Sharif Willis..." [164]

---

162. State of Minnesota v. Monterey T. Willis, C7-95-2705, Supreme Court, (February 13, 1997).

163. Brunswick, M., Leyden, P., & Diaz, K. (1992, November 25). 4th Haaf suspect turns self in. *Start Tribune.*

164. State of Minnesota v. Monterey T. Willis, C7-95-2705, Supreme Court, (February 13, 1997).

Even more damning, Pepi McKenzie testified that Sharif "ordered and planned the hit."[165] Police investigators had reason to believe Sharif was the fifth suspect and the one that got away. There was court testimony implicating him as the mastermind behind the killing. His nephew was one of the gunmen. The planning of the murder took place at Sharif's house. But prosecutors said they didn't have enough to convict him. Ellison's involvement with the surrender of Pepi McKenzie and his ties to Sharif and other Vice Lords members have often proved controversial. Ellison was a defense attorney back then. He has since maintained that while he helped arrange Pepi McKenzie's surrender, he never represented Sharif, his nephew Monterey, or any of the defendants charged in the killing of Officer Haaf. He has often pointed out that Sharif was never charged in that case.

## Ellison Defended Sharif Willis—and Lost

However, Ellison represented Sharif when he faced charges in another violent crime. On October 21, 1994, Sharif went on a week-long crack binge that came to a violent end when he held people at gunpoint inside a gas station in North Minneapolis. Sharif believed someone at the S & S repair shop stole two gold spinners from the rims on his Mercedes. Sharif hit one victim in the head, jumped on another, and ordered everyone to get down on the floor while threatening to "ice" them all with a Tec-9. Sharif had a 15-year-old accomplice. Sharif was supposed to be steering him away from violence, but he gave him a gun instead. Ellison was Sharif's defense attorney in this case. Although despite Ellison's efforts, Sharif was convicted on drugs and weapons charges and ultimately served 23 years in prison.[166] It doesn't seem like a case Ellison could forget.

---

165. Orrick, D. (2018, November 1). Keith Ellison, Louis Farrakhan, and 'cop killers': Smear campaign or fair game? *Pioneer Press.*

166. Worthington, R. (1992, February 21). In shadow of trial, faith in gang leader lies shattered. *Chicago Tribune.*

## Sharif Attends Arradondo's Swearing-in Ceremony

As if these coincidences weren't enough, the day before Arradondo was sworn in as the chief of police in 2017, church and community leaders held a press conference. They declared their support for Arradondo and took the opportunity to criticize the police union and its leadership (namely Bob). One of the more vocal leaders was Pastor McAfee, who founded United for Peace with Sharif Willis in 1992. There was also another coincidence the next day at Arradondo's swearing-in ceremony. Along with Arradondo's family, friends, and supporters, McAfee and Sharif were there. Sharif was sitting one row away from Bob. Sharif was likely the mastermind behind the execution of a Minneapolis police officer. He served 23 years in prison for a violent crime and was released just months before the ceremony. And he was welcomed at the milestone ceremony when Arradondo was sworn in as chief of the Minneapolis Police Department.

## The 2019 Arrest and Release of Sharif Willis

With all that history in mind, it might be easier to understand how Sharif was arrested in 2019 and almost immediately released for "lack of evidence." Sources with knowledge of that investigation (who did not want to be identified due to fear of retaliation), explained how Ellison, now the attorney general, stepped in and apparently made the charges against Sharif disappear.[167] This wasn't a parking ticket. This was a significant arrest based on a lengthy investigation. Sharif was supposed to be reformed for the second time. Although, given the crimes of revenge and retaliation he has been involved in, MPD officers were keeping an eye on him. Sharif was much older now, but apparently not wiser as he seemed to be going back to his old ways. When MPD officers carried out a search warrant where Sharif was residing, they found several rounds of ammunition and other evidence of criminal

---

167. Identity withheld (personal communication, July 17, 2022; July 21, 2022).

activity. It's illegal for ex-cons to have guns or ammunition, so Sharif was arrested and booked. Out of all the suspects arrested in that case, Sharif was the only one released in about the time it takes to read a police report. Supposedly, Freeman, the Hennepin County attorney, felt the evidence wasn't strong enough. But the fact that Sharif had Keith Ellison's business card on him when was arrested might have had something more to do with it.[168] Ellison couldn't keep Sharif out of prison years ago. But as the top cop in Minnesota, Ellison seemed to be making it up to him.

### Strong Ties and Strange Connections

If you're wondering how this relates to Derek Chauvin's trial, there are more than a few things to keep in mind. Ellison acted on behalf of various members of the Vice Lords back in the '90s, including Sharif Willis. Sharif's nephew, Monterey, was one of the four gang members arrested for killing Officer Jerry Haaf. Ellison escorted another suspect, Pepi McKenzie, back from Chicago to Minneapolis to be taken into custody. Ellison organized protests on behalf of the suspects, believing their rights were being violated by MPD and the criminal justice system back then. So just to be clear, Ellison was supporting members of the Vice Lords gang accused of killing a cop in cold blood. But now, Ellison was the lead prosecutor in a case involving George Floyd—an "unarmed Black man" allegedly murdered by cops. Ellison was no longer a defense attorney representing gang members; he was the attorney general. So, it's not difficult to imagine how Ellison might have been driven by rivalry, if not revenge. As Cindy Haaf, the daughter of slain officer Jerry Haaf explained, "Ellison never flipped sides, he always seemed to do more for criminals and not enough for law and order."[169] Ellison's sense of justice seems to have been

---

168. Identity withheld (personal communication, July 18, 2022).

169. Williams, R. (2022, September 30). Officer Jerry Haaf's daughter speaks out against parole for his murderers. *Alpha News*.

formed long ago. In response to protests after the second day of the L.A. riots in 1992, Ellison proclaimed:[170]

> "Black people do not live under democracy... You don't have an obligation to obey a government that considers you to be less than human."

*A monument that once marked the center of "George Floyd Square" (Source: Dr. JC Chaix). According to Crime Watch Minneapolis, nine homicides, including the fatal shooting of a pregnant woman, occurred within George Floyd Square or "The Free State of George Floyd" between May 26, 2020 and August 14, 2022.*

170. Brunswick, M., Leyden, P., & Diaz, K. (1992, May 1). At rallies in Twin Cities, many decry injustices while police aim to reassure. *Star Tribune.*

## Gangs & George Floyd's Funeral

This might have seemed like a trip down memory lane. But it's a necessary one. Ellison, Freeman, Willis, and McAfee isn't the name of a law firm. It's a list of some of the key players who have been involved with crime in Minneapolis for decades, on one side or another. They were around when Minneapolis was "Murderapolis" due to all the gang violence, and still around for the trial of Derek Chauvin. Their influence and involvement showed up in some strange ways during the trial—even during George Floyd's funeral.

The funeral began with opening remarks by Pastor Jerry McAfee, which were significant. But not so much in a profound way, more in a way like gang signs and gang territories. Pastor McAfee began George Floyd's funeral by saying:[171]

> "On behalf of the pastors and preachers from Minneapolis and
> St. Paul, the Blood's on the South side, Gangster Disciples and
> Vice Lords on the North side, Psalm 27."

The funeral was broadcasted live by TV news stations everywhere, including WCCO. But if you ask anybody about how George Floyd's funeral began with a pastor giving a shout out to street gangs followed by a reading from Psalm 27, they'd probably think you've lost your mind. Although that's what *exactly* happened. Pastor McAfee called out the Bloods, the Gangster Disciples, and the Vice Lords—the same gang whose members turned to Ellison for support or legal representation back in the day. Sharif Willis was one of them. Given his association with the Vice Lords—one of the gangs mentioned during Floyd's funeral—it's insane to think Ellison would even dare to claim that he was impartial. It's also crazy to think that Ellison and Freeman could cooperate given their twisted history and affiliations. The fact that Freeman and Ellison

---

171. Watch the memorial for George Floyd live from Minneapolis. (June 4, 2020). *WRAL*. https://www.wral.com/19130032/; CNN Live Event/Special: Soon memorial service Minneapolis for George Floyd; Memorial service for George Floyd, aired 2:30-3pm ET. (2020, June 4). *CNN*. http://edition.cnn.com/TRANSCRIPTS/2006/04/se.02.html

didn't recuse themselves from Chauvin's trial seemed like an ethics violation waiting to happen. But it never did.

### Rivalry, Dysfunction and Prosecution

The dysfunction between Ellison and Freeman is another issue that likely had a negative effect on Chauvin's trial. For example, after reviewing the autopsy report, Freeman seemed reluctant to charge Chauvin with murder. The criminal complaint he wrote seemed more like an argument about why charges should *not* be filed. Days later, Governor Walz stepped in and announced that Ellison was taking over the case. Just 48 hours later, charges against Chauvin were upgraded. The timing seemed obvious. Much like the way Freeman silently stood next to Ellison during a press conference—and then left the room when Ellison started answering questions from the press.[172] Maybe Freeman changed his mind about charging Chauvin, or maybe he was coerced by his former rival. Whatever the case may have been, Freeman seemed to be following orders and ignoring what others had to say. Four other Hennepin County attorneys did not want to file charges against the other three officers and withdrew from the case. One of them was Amy Sweasy. She thought the charges against Kueng, Lane, and Thao were unethical, so, she withdrew from the case. She also filed a complaint against Freeman due to workplace discrimination. In her complaint, Sweasy wrote:

> "I believed the charges (Freeman) recommended violated professional and ethical rules and I withdrew from the case."

Sweasy also stated that Freeman retaliated against her for not wanting to charge the other officers. Sweasy didn't have a pro-police agenda. In fact, she helped to successfully prosecute former MPD Officer Mohamed Noor, who shot and killed a woman for no apparent reason as she approached his police

---

172. Montemayor, S. (2020, June 17). Latest chapter of Keith Ellison and Mike Freeman's partnership could define their careers. *Star Tribune*.

car. Ultimately, the Minnesota Department of Human Rights issued no official finding of judgment against Freeman, but the Hennepin County Board approved a promotion and a payment of $190,000 to settle Sweasy's complaint.[173] All of this might seem confusing and overwhelming. Which is precisely the issue: there was so much dysfunction and such a lack of ethical conduct and impartiality that four prosecutors withdrew from the case.

## Ellison's "Team of Michael Jordans" (& Their Trick Plays)

Even without four prosecutors, Ellison was hardly at a loss in prosecuting Chauvin. When Ellison said he would use every resource available to convict him, he apparently meant it. Ellison had 14 other attorneys handling the prosecution, enough for a basketball team.[174] Which, is what Ellison called them. The prosecution was a team of "Michael Jordans" because every one of them was a "superstar."[175] If so, then Chauvin's trial seemed like a game of 15 on 1. Counting himself, Ellison had 15 attorneys working on behalf of the government in prosecuting Derek Chauvin. Who knows how many assistants they had, but they took up two floors of the Hennepin County courthouse. All of them were working against defense attorney Eric Nelson, who was handling practically all the duties during the trial by himself. Of course, the media and the Left realized the defense was outnumbered. They were doing their part to downplay the number of prosecutors in the case. Nelson didn't feel outnumbered per se, but he did say, "There's no way the jury didn't notice the difference."[176]

---

173. Gockowski, A. (2022, May 31). Court filing: Four prosecutors opposed charging Chauvin's partners. *Alpha News*.

174. Salter, J. (2021, April 4). Explainer: Legion of Chauvin prosecutors, each with own role. *AP News*.

175. Ortiz, E. (2021, April 21). Prosecutors in Chauvin trial had a winning strategy. Here's what they did right. *NBC News*.

176. E. Nelson (personal communication July 19, 2022).

## Outnumbered, "Overblown," & A $27-Million Settlement

At times, the number of prosecutors involved in the trial became embarrassingly clear. For example, in what seemed like repeated attempts to influence the jury, prosecutors kept mentioning how the family of George Floyd received $27 million from the city to settle the lawsuit filed by Ben Crump.[177] The settlement was announced during jury selection. Even *The New York Times* seemed concerned about how the settlement could influence the jury.[178] Judge Cahill warned the prosecution several times to stop mentioning it during the trial. Prosecutor Schleicher pushed his luck one too many times. Judge Cahill interrupted him. While giving the prosecution yet another warning, he asked: "How many lawyers are… working for the state in this case, Mr. Schleicher? Is it 10, 12?"

Schleicher admitted: "I don't have that number, your honor…"

To think the jury didn't take note of the settlement or the number of prosecutors after that embarrassing exchange seems ridiculous. Schleicher said the concerns were "overblown," although two jurors were dismissed because they admittedly could no longer be impartial because of the settlement.[179] There were other issues with jurors as well. Ellison and the prosecution seemed to be creating unfair advantages and undermining impartiality by mentioning the settlement and concealing the number of prosecutors who were involved. Apparently, they were also using other tricks and tactics.

---

177. The case was filed by Crump and co-counsel Antonio Romanucci. Crump said it was "the largest pre-trial settlement of a wrongful death lawsuit in US history." See Allen, J. (2021, March 12). George Floyd's family receives $27 million settlement from Minneapolis over his death. *Reuters*.

178. Bogel-Burroughs, N., & Eligon, J. (March 13, 2021). A $27 million settlement for George Floyd's family could influence jurors, *The New York Times*.

179. Allen, J. (2021, March 17). Two jurors dismissed in trial on Floyd's death after $27 million settlement, two new ones seated. *Reuters*.

## Creating Conflicts of Interest

For example, the cause of George Floyd's death was pivotal. The autopsy report was certainly open to interpretation. But to establish reasonable doubt, the defense needed a second opinion, if not several. During a typical trial, the prosecution calls their witnesses, and the defense calls theirs. In this case, Chauvin's defense attorney didn't seem to have much of a chance to call on qualified expert witnesses. That's because Ellison and his legion of prosecutors and assistants apparently created conflicts of interest. Not to get into all the details, but a witness must testify on behalf of one side or another, not both. Doing so would create a conflict of interest. Likewise, if the prosecution contacts a witness first, it would be a conflict for that witness to speak with the defense.

Lane had watched Chauvin's trial and noticed the prosecution had 300-400 people on their witness list, but only 30 or so testified.[180] They had all these people, like medical examiners on their list just to create conflicts, so the defense couldn't call them. When Nelson tried to contact several leading medical examiners to testify for the defense, they all declared a conflict of interest—because someone already contacted them. Nelson wasn't sure who it was. But the conflicts made it practically impossible for the defense to get a qualified second opinion. Any hope of expert testimony to counter the prosecution barely stood a chance. One might expect this kind of manipulation during a divorce case—not a criminal jury trial led by a state attorney general.

## Hay Stacking

The prosecution apparently also used other less-than-ethical and hardly professional tactics as well, including "hay stacking." Hay stacking involves deliberately making it difficult for the other side to sort out documents and

---

180. Actually 38 witnesses testified for the prosecution during Chauvin's trial; Walsh, P., Simons, A., & Sayle, H. (2021, April 15). Who were the witnesses in the Derek Chauvin trial? *Star Tribune.*

evidence, much like looking for a needle in a haystack. Along with delivering documents in disarray, another bratty move involves delivering evidence without giving the other side enough time to make sense of it. Like delivering piles of written evidence less than 30 minutes before court is scheduled to begin. On more than one occasion, Nelson was left scrambling to sort out hundreds, if not thousands of pages. Sure, things like this might happen occasionally. But Ellison and his prosecution team were doing this repeatedly. In fact, Nelson complained to the court about it. Nelson pointed out how in one instance, the prosecution received files of digital evidence from BCA investigators that were meticulously organized on a disk drive. Instead of sharing the files with Nelson in the same neatly organized format, the prosecution gave Nelson a single 6,000-page digital file. Making things even worse, the file wasn't organized and pages from one file were mixed in with another. The file also wasn't searchable. So, even if Nelson figured out what he was looking for, he couldn't search the massive document to find it.

Consequently, Nelson had to spend more than 150 hours printing and sorting out the documents by hand. The prosecution did this repeatedly, as Nelson wrote in his sworn complaint.[181] Jurors typically aren't aware of underhanded tricks since hay stacking isn't something that's obvious in the courtroom. Likewise, the media and the Left seemed to be doing everything possible to dismiss even the slightest criticisms about the prosecution. I witnessed this firsthand at WCCO. When I first came across the issue of hay stacking, I thought it was newsworthy, especially since prosecutors seemed to be resorting to such childish conduct in a high-profile case. But like so many other news outlets, WCCO ignored it.

---

181. Affidavit of Eric J. Nelson. State of Minnesota v. Derek Chauvin, 27-CR-20-12646 (January 26, 2021).

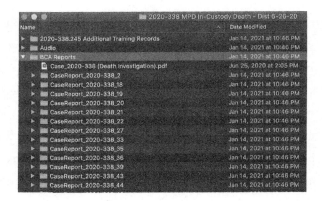

*(Top) A screenshot of the well-organized, searchable digital files the prosecution team received. The prosecution did not share the same digital files, but one massive, unsearchable file that defense attorney Eric Nelson had to print and sort by hand. (Bottom) These are just some of the boxes related to MPD training. (Affidavit of Eric J. Nelson. State of Minnesota v. Derek Chauvin, 27-CR-20-12646 (January 26, 2021).*

## Questionable Evidence & Testimony

Along with questionable jury instructions and unethical conduct, a lot of questionable testimony was offered during the trial. More than a few witnesses, and even the prosecution, were apparently lying by omission. Although, perhaps more than any other witness, the testimony of Chief Arradondo seemed to be the most untruthful and most controversial.

### Chief Arradondo & The Most Controversial Testimony of All

Depending upon how you look at it, no matter what Arradondo had to say, his testimony was going to seem questionable. His own prejudice made it that way. On June 22, 2020, just weeks after the arrest and death of George Floyd, Arradondo already declared that Chauvin was guilty of murder:[182]

> "Mr. George Floyd's tragic death was not due to a lack of training—the training was there. Chauvin knew what he was doing. I agree with Attorney General Ellison: what happened to Mr. Floyd was murder."

After a making a statement like that, it would be foolish to expect that Arradondo could be an impartial, unbiased witness. At first Arradondo fielded softball questions about use of force, policies, and training. Prosecutor Schleicher then asked Arradondo about Derek Chauvin's actions. That's when Arradondo's testimony started to unravel and seem fabricated and bizarre. For example, in discussing neck restraints that police might use, Arradondo explained:

---

182. Minneapolis Police Chief on George Floyd Death: 'This was murder—it wasn't a lack of training,' (2020, June 22). *Fox 9 KMSP*.

"Conscious neck restraint by policy mentions light to moderate pressure. When I look at exhibit 17, and when I look at the facial expression of Mr. Floyd, that does not appear in any way, shape or form that is light to moderate pressure…"

### Facial Expressions—A New Standard of Use of Force?

Facial expressions hardly seem like reliable indicators of use of force. Not to be insensitive but comparing a snapshot from Thomas Lane's body cam video with Exhibit 17 shows how Arradondo's claim could easily be mistaken. Floyd made similar facial expressions when police officers first approached him—and weren't even touching him.

*George Floyd exhibited a facial expression similar to Exhibit 17. Derek Chauvin was not even at the scene and was not touching or applying force to him at the time, neither was any other police officer.*

*An excerpt from the viral cellphone video known as Exhibit 17, which was shown dozens of times during the trial, as if to create a memory of it in the jurors' minds. Chief Arradondo testified that he could tell the amount of pressure Chauvin was exerting based on George Floyd's facial expression. Note how this image frames and isolates Chauvin and does not show any of the other officers who were involved.*

## A Different Kind of Police Oversight

During cross-examination, Nelson asked Chief Arradondo about the use of force. Nelson then submitted Exhibit 1020 to the court. It was a side-by-side comparison of viral cellphone video and Officer Kueng's police body cam video. Nelson then asked Arradondo about the comparison:[183]

> "From the perspective of Ms. Frazier's camera, it appears that Officer Chauvin's knee is on the neck of Mr. Floyd."

Arradondo replied, "Yes."

Nelson then asked,

> "Would you agree that from the perspective of Officer Kueng's body camera it appears that Officer Chauvin's knee was more on Mr. Floyd's shoulder blade?"

Chief Arradondo hesitated, but then said: "Yes."

Nelson then concluded, "I have no further questions."

After Nelson was finished, Schleicher began his cross-examination by asking Arradondo:

> "And so the knee of the defendant was on Mr. Floyd's neck up until the time you just pointed out.

Arradondo then gave an answer that could not possibly be true according to his own admission:

> "Yes. When I view that video portion, that is the first time that I've seen the knee of the defendant on the shoulder blade area."

---

183. Pagones, S. (2021, April 6). Ex-Minneapolis police officer Chauvin was trained twice in past 4 years to diffuse tense situations: testimony. *Fox News*.

If this was the "first time" Arradondo had seen Chauvin's knee on Floyd's shoulder blade area, then it seems Arradondo didn't review the body cam videos too closely. Or maybe he never watched them at all. Maybe he didn't need to, since he already made up his mind that this was a "murder," as he told the media. Maybe Arradondo was lying by omission, or limiting his answers during testimony, or failing to be a true leader by overlooking the facts for the sake of self-righteousness. Whatever he might have been up to, the jury seems to have believed his testimony. But this wasn't the first time that Arradondo seemed to be caught off guard and corrected himself.

Just hours after the arrest and death of George Floyd, Bob asked Arradondo about the body cam footage. Arradondo kept saying he made the decision to call in the FBI. However, in his statement to FBI and BCA investigators days later, Arradondo spoke as if he went off script:[184]

> "...I had also obviously, *we*—I had made the decision to have BCA here. But then I contacted our FBI..."

The switch between "we" and "I" says a lot about what Arradondo was thinking, and maybe even more about what he was supposed to say. Apparently, as the use of "we" suggests, Arradondo most likely didn't make the decision by himself. During the interview with the BCA and FBI, Arradondo explained that after Bob and the other union leaders left, he spent the early morning hours:

> "...contacting local faith leaders, community activists, community leaders, from the African American community... forecasting that because we did not... own the video that was out there."

---

184. Chief Arradondo was interviewed by BCA Special Agent James Reyerson and FBI Special Agent Blake Hostetter on June 11, 2020; Minnesota Department of Public Safety, Bureau of Criminal Apprehension (BCA) Case #2020-338; emphasis added.

MPD may not have "owned" the video that was out there, but they certainly had the police body cam videos and could have reviewed and released them. Arradondo was the Deputy Chief when the Jamar Clark shooting took place—and Ellison and BLM activists demanded the release of video footage. He must have known he was about to repeat the same mistakes. Arradondo could have reviewed and released the body cam videos. But he didn't. The fact that Arradondo called leaders and activists indicates his priorities. These conversations might have been more of a political PR move for his own benefit. Whatever Arradondo said seemed to have worked because they immediately absolved him of any wrongdoing. Arradondo then told the BCA investigator that he based *his* decisions, the ones he supposedly made on his own, solely upon the viral video—not the police body cam footage. What Arradondo said on the witness stand contradicted what he said during his previous interview with BCA and FBI agents, and vice versa. So, one way or another, Arradondo apparently didn't know the truth, wasn't telling the truth, or wasn't letting the truth be told.

## What Training?

While there were plenty of "experts" who testified about the policies and training of MPD officers, Chief Arradondo's testimony on the topic seems the most suspicious. One might expect that as the chief of police, Arradondo could recognize the policies and training of his own department. But this didn't seem to be the case. For example, when questioned by the prosecution about Exhibit 17, Arradondo testified:

> "That is not part of our policy, that is not what we teach and that should not be condoned..."

Let's give Arradondo the benefit of the doubt. Besides, if anyone should be able to recognize MPD training techniques, it would be the person in charge of MPD training. That would be Inspector Katie Blackwell. She was in charge of the Minneapolis Police training division when George Floyd was arrested and died. She also testified during Chauvin's trial. When the prosecution asked her about how Chauvin and the other officers were trying to restrain Floyd, she testified:[185]

> "I don't know what kind of improvised position that is. So that's not what we train."

While that sounds perfectly reasonable, it doesn't seem like Inspector Blackwell knows how MPD officers are trained—or maybe she was lying. The procedure the four officers were following was and still is part of MPD training. It was clearly written in MPD policy. To be a bit more specific, again, it's policy 5-316, "Maximal Restraint Technique."

---

185. Romo, V. (2021, April 5). Former training commander on Chauvin neck restraint: 'That's not what we train.' *NPR*.

27-CR-20-12951

Filed in District C
State of Minne
7/7/2020 11:0(

## Mechanics of a Neck Restraint

- Secure the **Neck Brace Principle**
  - Stabilization of the head & neck
  - Protection of the Trachea & Airway *(front of throat)*
- Break the SUB's balance to the rear
- Compress veins, arteries, nerves & muscles of the neck
- SUB resisting produces the Valsalva Maneuver *(straining against a closed glottis)*

Drills: partner up, demonstrate by the numbers, single arm, switch arm, figure four, short arm, switch partners, defense to neck restraint, circle up with partners, rotate outer partner for 10 reps

## Maximal Restraint Technique Application

**5-316    MAXIMAL RESTRAINT TECHNIQUE** (05/29/02) (06/13/14) (07/13/17) (04/02/18)

(B-C)

**I.    PURPOSE**
To establish a policy on the use of "hobble restraint devices" and the method of transporting prisoners who have been handcuffed with a hobble restraint applied.

**II.    POLICY**
The hobble restraint device may be used to carry out the Maximal Restraint Technique, consistent with training offered by the Minneapolis Police Department on the use of the Maximal Restraint Technique and the Use of Force Policy.

**III.    DEFINITIONS**
**Hobble Restraint Device:** A device that limits the motion of a person by tethering both legs together. Ripp Hobble ™ is the only authorized brand to be used.
**Maximal Restraint Technique (MRT):** Technique used to secure a subject's feet to their waist in order to prevent the movement of legs and limit the possibility of property damage or injury to him/her or others.
**Prone Position:** For purposes of this policy, the term Prone Position means to lay a restrained subject face down on their chest.
**Side Recovery Position:** Placing a restrained subject on their side in order to reduce pressure on his/her chest and facilitate breathing.

**IV.    RULES/REGULATIONS**
   **A.  Maximal Restraint Technique – Use (06/13/14)**
      1.  The Maximal Restraint Technique shall only be used in situations where handcuffed subjects are combative and still pose a threat to themselves, officers or others, or could cause significant damage to property if not properly restrained.

      2.  Using the hobble restraint device, the MRT is accomplished in the following manner:
        a.  One hobble restraint device is placed around the subject's waist.
        b.  A second hobble restraint device is placed around the subject's feet.

*A copy of the Minnesota Police Department Policy Number 5-316, Maximal Restraint Technique, as submitted as "Defense Exhibit 7" as part of Derek Chauvin's trial. The dates next to the title indicate when the policy was established and revised.*

27-CR-20-12951

Filed in District Court
State of Minnesota
7/7/2020 11:00 AM

    c.  Connect the hobble restraint device around the feet to the hobble restraint device around the waist in front of the subject.

    d.  **Do not** tie the feet of the subject directly to their hands behind their back. This is also known as a hogtie.

3.  A supervisor shall be called to the scene where a subject has been restrained using the MRT to evaluate the manner in which the MRT was applied and to evaluate the method of transport.

**B.  Maximal Restraint Technique – Safety (06/13/14)**

1.  As soon as reasonably possible, any person restrained using the MRT who is in the prone position shall be placed in the following positions based on the type of restraint used:

    a.  If the hobble restraint device is used, the person shall be placed in the side recovery position.

2.  When using the MRT, an EMS response should be considered.

3.  Under no circumstances, shall a subject restrained using the MRT be transported in the prone position.

4.  Officers shall monitor the restrained subject until the arrival of medical personnel, if necessary, or transfer to another agency occurs.

5.  In the event any suspected medical conditions arise prior to transport, officers will notify paramedics and request a medical evaluation of the subject or transport the subject immediately to a hospital.

6.  A prisoner under Maximal Restraint should be transported by a two-officer squad, when feasible. The restrained subject shall be seated upright, unless it is necessary to transport them on their side. The MVR should be activated during transport, when available.

7.  Officers shall also inform the person who takes custody of the subject that the MRT was applied.

**C.  Maximal Restraint Technique – Reporting (06/13/14)**

1.  Anytime the hobble restraint device is used, officers' Use of Force reporting shall document the circumstances requiring the use of the restraint and the technique applied, regardless of whether an injury was incurred.

2.  Supervisors shall complete a Supervisor's Force Review.

3.  When the Maximal Restraint Technique is used, officers' report shall document the following:

    ·  How the MRT was applied, listing the hobble restraint device as the implement used.

    ·  The approximate amount of time the subject was restrained.

    ·  How the subject was transported and the position of the subject.

    ·  Observations of the subject's physical and physiological actions (examples include: significant changes in behavior, consciousness or medical issues).

### Ground Defense 101

**Break Falls** *(Falling Backwards to a Defensive Ground Position)*

- Start in low squat, arms crossed with hands on shoulders, chin tucked
  - Roll backward until your back contacts the ground
  - As you contact the ground, exhale & palm-slap the ground (arms extended out like a "t")
- Roll back up to a seated Defensive Ground Position
  - Post up on gun side hand/ bend opposite leg & plant foot

*A copy of the Minnesota Police Department Policy Number 5-316, IV. B.1., Maximal Restraint Technique, as submitted as "Defense Exhibit 7" as part of Derek Chauvin's trial.*

Sections I and II of policy 5-316 refer to "hobble restraint devices." It's difficult to imagine how Inspector Blackwell, who was in charge of training, didn't recognize this policy. The same goes for Chief Arradondo, and Lieutenant Johnny Mercil, who also testified about use of force and related issues during the trial. They said they didn't recognize the "position" or the "technique" from the exhibits they were shown by the prosecution. Maybe if they watched the police body cam videos, they would have known better.

At least they might have heard the officers referring to "restraints" and "hobble." They would have heard Lane asking Kueng, "You got hobble?" They would have heard Lane tell Thao, "Mine's on my side. It's listed, it's labelled. It says hobble." They would have seen Thao give Lane the "hobble" restraint straps. They would have heard the officers request an ambulance, which was another textbook example of following MRT procedure. And they would have seen how they decided not to fully restrain Floyd with the "hobble" restraints. In other words, they would have seen how the officers de-escalated and were waiting for the ambulance to arrive, which also follows policy 5-316. Granted, just because Maximal Restraint Technique was written in policy doesn't mean it was part of MPD training. After all, Chief Arradondo testified, "That is not what we teach."[186] Inspector Blackwell said basically the same thing: "That's not what we train." However, MPD had a specific lesson plan regarding use of force that included "when and how to apply the Maximal Restraint Technique (MRT)." Also, the in-service training that was mandatory for all officers in 2019, included training about MRT.

---

186. "'That is not what we teach': Mpls. police chief Arradondo says Derek Chauvin's actions violated dept. policies," *WCCO, CBS Minnesota,* (April 5, 2021).

# MRT – Use (5-316)

Only used in situations where subject is:
  Handcuffed & combative and
    — Poses threat to self/other, or
    — Could cause significant damage to property if not
      restrained.

MRT application:
  One Hobble around ankles
  One Hobble around waist
  Connect hobble from ankles to waist **IN FRONT** of
  subject.

010596

*A presentation slide from the "2019 Defensive Tactics In-Service Phase 3" training provided to all MPD officers about the use of the Maximal Restraint Technique (MRT). Exhibit 15. State of Minnesota v. Derek Chauvin, 27-CR-20-12646 (August 28, 2020).*

So MRT was part of MPD policy and was also part of the training given to all officers in 2019. With that in mind, it doesn't seem like Blackwell, Arradondo, Mercil, and other so-called expert witnesses, were telling the truth. It seems more like they were lying by omission, if not lying outright. Chauvin's mother, Carolyn, will be the first to tell you she's no expert on police procedures. However, even she realized how their testimony didn't match what was obviously written down in policy and training materials:[187]

> "I just don't understand how they can be so dishonest. It's right there in the policy manual."

---

187. C. Pawlenty (personal communication, September 4, 2022).

Being skeptical is a good thing. It's necessary for civility, democracy, and a free and mindful press. So, at some point, anyone wondering about the contradictions between MPD policy, and the testimony of Arradondo, Blackwell, Mercil, and others should be asking "Why would they lie?" It's a good question and a necessary one. Unfortunately, the answer doesn't bode well for police and city leaders. That's because policy "5-316, Maximal Restraint Technique" has an obvious flaw.

I would never claim to be an expert on policing by any means. Even Bob, who has been dealing with this stuff for decades, often looks to experts for advice. But the flaw is obvious. Policy 5-316.4.B.1 reads:[188]

> "As soon as reasonably possible, any person restrained using the MRT who is in the prone position shall be placed in the following positions based on the type of restraint used:
>
> a. If the hobble restraint device is used, the person shall be placed in the side recovery position.

So, if the hobble is used, the person "shall be" placed in the side recovery position. However, the policy does *not* say what to do if the hobble is *not* used, which is what happened during the arrest of George Floyd. The officers intended to use a hobble, but de-escalated and did not. Therefore, there was no mandate about the side recovery position if a hobble was *not* used. This boils down to one simple fact. Chauvin, Kueng, Lane, and Thao were clearly following policy 5-316—despite what others may have testified.

---

188. Minnesota Police Department Policy Number 5-316, IV. B.1., Maximal Restraint Technique, as submitted as "Defense Exhibit 7" as part of Derek Chauvin's trial.

## An Unfortunate Recap

Admittedly, this barely scratches the surface of what went on during Derek Chauvin's trial and all the politics, rivalries, and circumstances beneath it all. It's also not even a fraction of what Kueng, Lane, and Thao went through in their cases. So much more of the truth remains to be told, but here are some of the unfortunate consequences caused by all the lies.

### Derek Chauvin

Former police officer Derek Chauvin was arrested on May 29, 2020. He was originally charged with third-degree murder and manslaughter. When Attorney General Keith Ellison took over the case at the request of Governor Walz, the charges were upgraded. Almost a year later, the trial of the *State of Minnesota v. Derek Chauvin* began on March 8, 2021. On April 20th, the jury found him guilty of unintentional second-degree murder, guilty of third-degree murder, and guilty of second-degree manslaughter. During the trial, the DOJ was lying in wait. The federal government had plans to arrest Chauvin *in court* for civil-rights violations if he was acquitted. The day after Chauvin was found guilty, US Attorney General Merrick Garland revealed the hand the federal government had been waiting to play:[189]

> "...the Justice Department has opened a civil investigation to determine whether the Minneapolis Police Department engages in a pattern or practice of unconstitutional or unlawful policing."

Chauvin was sentenced to 22 years and 6 months in prison on June 25, 2021. In December 2021, he pled guilty in federal court to civil rights violations related to "unreasonable force" concerning two separate incidents. One was the arrest and death of George Floyd, and the other was related to an incident that

---

189. Wallace, D. (2021, April 21). Derek Chauvin conviction: DOJ reportedly had 'secret' plan to arrest ex-cop if acquitted. *Fox News*.

occurred in 2017.[190] After Chauvin was convicted, he was moved to the maximum-security prison in Minnesota. For 23 hours a day, he was kept in a 10-by-10-foot cell with just a bench, mattress pad, a shower, and combination toilet/sink. Chauvin was not allowed to have much of anything else; books, papers, TV, radio, none of the things we take for granted. Guards checked on him day and night, every 30 minutes for his safety.[191] On August 24, 2022, Chauvin was moved to a federal prison in Arizona and will be held with less restrictive conditions to serve out his sentence. He has since filed an appeal.

### The Fate of "The Other Three"

Like Chauvin, former officers Kueng, Lane, and Thao also faced state and federal charges. They faced the same judge and the same lead prosecutor as Chauvin; Judge Cahill and Attorney General Keith Ellison.[192] They also faced charges in federal court for violating George Floyd's civil rights. They were each found guilty in February 2022. On July 27, 2022, Kueng and Thao were sentenced in federal court. Kueng was sentenced to three years. Thao was sentenced to three years and six months. They were also sentenced to serve two years of supervised release when they are released from prison.[193]

### Thomas Lane: Finding a Means to an End

Just three days before he was dispatched to a 911 call and encountered George Floyd, Lane had finally completed field training. He texted his wife that day to tell her he was happy to have "finally found what he was supposed to be doing with his life" and thanked her. Lane wanted to help people, make a

---

190. Former Minneapolis Police officer Derek Chauvin pleads guilty in federal court to depriving George Floyd and a minor victim of their constitutional rights. (2021, December 15). *United States Department of Justice, Office of Public Affairs.*

191. D. Chauvin (personal communication, August 8, 2022); see also McEvoy, J. (2021, April 21). Derek Chauvin being kept in solitary confinement at maximum-security prison. *Forbes.*

192. The state cases were pending at the time I was writing this in October 2022.

193. Due to their on-going cases and likely appeals, I can only respect the requests of their attorneys to avoid discussing their cases in more detail.

difference, and do something that mattered. He was willing to fight the charges in state and federal court. His defense attorney, Earl Gray, was eager to fight as well. Gray insisted this case was the most disgusting perversion of justice he'd ever seen. Even in July 2020, just about a month after Judge Cahill lifted the gag order, Gray insisted:[194]

> "None of these guys—even Chauvin—actually killed him [George Floyd]. He killed himself."

Gray also knew that in the federal case, the prosecution would have to prove that Lane *willfully* intended to kill and violate George Floyd's rights. This required more than just proving intent. Nonetheless, it would likely involve more time for trial preparation, longer and more complicated trials in state and federal court, and lengthy, complicated appeals. With all that in mind, Lane decided not to fight. His decision was based on a lot of soul-searching and watching what happened during Chauvin's trial. But ultimately, he said his decision to plead guilty was because he "wanted to be a part of his newborn baby's life" sooner rather than later.

Lane pled guilty to avoid a lengthy trial and all the appeals. He said he wanted to put everything behind him hopefully before the time toddlers start forming their first memories. Whatever activists and police "reformers" make of his plea, it doesn't change the facts or suddenly make the accusations true. For Lane, a guilty plea was a means to an end. As part of the plea arrangement between state and federal prosecutors, Lane pled guilty and was sentenced two years and six months in prison.

---

194. Read, R. (2020, August 20). Attorney for Minneapolis police officer says he'll argue George Floyd died of an overdose and a heart condition. *Los Angeles Times*.

## We've Heard a Lot, But Have We Heard the Truth?

"I'm here because of politics and perceived racism." That's what Derek Chauvin told corrections officers when he was arrested in May 2020. His dry sense of humor broke the tension for a moment. Unfortunately, he probably didn't realize how prophetic his remark would prove to be.

If you don't ask the right questions, you won't get the right answers. That's how it works in journalism—and that's how it works in court. With that in mind, the trial of Derek Chauvin shows how the right questions were never asked. There's often more than just "two sides" to a story. The same can be said for court cases where there's often at least four sides involved. There's what one side says, what the other says, what they prove in court—and then there's the truth.

We've heard the prosecution.

We've heard the defense.

We've heard the instructions to the jury and their verdict.

But that doesn't mean we've actually heard the truth.

# PART VI

## THE RIGHT SIDE OF HISTORY?

## The Right Side of History?

On June 10, 2020, Chief Arradondo told the media:[195]

> "History is being written now and I'm determined to make sure we are on the right side of history."

Being on the right side of history was supposedly all about demanding "justice" for George Floyd and just about everything else during the riots in Minneapolis. However, along with the guilty verdicts, the riots, and defunding the police, many attempts to be on "the right side of history" have gone very wrong. There have been epic failures of leadership from the White House to the mayor's office in Minneapolis and everywhere in between.

Crime has skyrocketed.

Police departments have become dangerously understaffed.

And civility and law and order no longer seem to exist.

But if we're ever going to make sense of the aftermath we've inherited, questioning the "leaders" who claimed to be on "the right side of history" seems like a good place to start. So, I've taken some of them to task—on their own terms, according to their own words and deeds—even though they declined or did not respond to my requests for interviews.

---

195. MPR News Staff. (2020, June 10). Floyd killing: Chief vows changes to put police on 'right side of history.' *MPR News.*

## Chief Medaria Arradondo

Chief Arradondo had a profound influence on the Minneapolis Police Department and the city of Minneapolis, but not in a good way. He boldly spoke out against "police misconduct" and condemned the death of George Floyd as a "murder"—before ever watching the body cam videos. He also promised to build a new system of policing for the sake of being on the right side of history.

However, Arradondo was already on the wrong side of history. Record-breaking crime had emerged even before the riots. In 2019, people in Minneapolis seemed deeply concerned, as survey results revealed:[196]

> "I was going to live downtown, then decided not to because of the gun shots and violence."

> "Downtown has become extremely unsafe over the past few years due to lack of police presence and high tolerance for intimidating behavior."

> "Don't lose control of our city. It will be a MUCH more difficult task to take back."

In 2020, six months after the riots, Arradondo admitted that criminals were only "emboldened" as shootings reached a five-year high.[197] A year after the riots, violence was out of control. With rampant lawlessness and a depleted police department, citizens were desperately pleading with police and city leaders to do something:[198]

---

196. Results summary, 2019 perception survey, (2020, February 6). *Minneapolis DID Budget and Operations Committee.*

197. Keith, T. (2020, September 15). Minneapolis council members air frustrations as shootings reach 5-year high. *Fox 9 News.*

198. Glover, M. (2020, September 14). Community concerned over increased gun violence in Minneapolis' Jordan neighborhood. *Fox 9 News.*

"This is a cry for help. I need someone to come and tell us we have something better to look forward to."

That "someone" was *not* Arradondo. Apparently, he was secretly preparing his departure as a finalist to take over as police chief in San Jose, California.[199] He dropped out of the running in January 2021, about the same time he apparently gave up his promise of building a new future for the Minneapolis Police Department. By the end of the year, Arradondo announced his retirement and made a quiet exit when his term ended in January 2022. According to practically every measure, Arradondo left the department and the city in shambles. He claimed to be an agent of change and reform. He was hailed as a hero by community leaders and the media. Arradondo was basically given a free pass despite his catastrophic failures. In case anybody was wondering which side of history Arradondo was on, the facts speak for themselves.

---

199. Ibrahim, M. (2021, December 6). Minneapolis' first black police chief, Arradondo to retire," *Associated Press*.

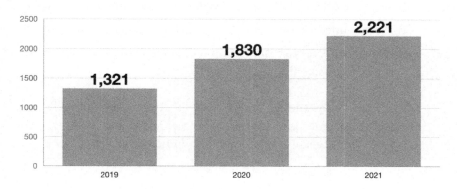

### Robberies Under Chief Arradondo's "Leadership"

*The number of robberies during the last three years of Chief Arradondo's tenure as Chief of the Minneapolis Police Department, 2019-2021 (Source: Minneapolis Crime Dashboard).*

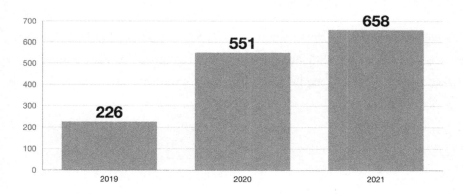

### Gunshot Wound Victims: Under Chief Arradondo's "Leadership"

*The number of gunshot wound victims during the last three years of Chief Arradondo's tenure, 2019-2021 (Source: Minneapolis Crime Dashboard).*

## City Council Member Jeremiah Ellison

Jeremiah Ellison, a member of the Minneapolis City Council, was outspoken about police reform after the death of George Floyd. He too envisioned long overdue police reform. Jeremiah often touted equality and socialist ideas. Even his official bio echoes Marxist tendencies:[200]

> "We need to tip the scales of power between the publicly funded, uniformly trained police force and the racially + economically diverse, collective of individuals that make up a neighborhood."

Just days after the riots began, Jeremiah publicly declared his "official support for ANTIFA" on Twitter:[201]

> "I hereby declare, officially, my support for ANTIFA. Unless someone can prove to me ANTIFA is behind the burning of black and immigrant owned businesses in my ward, I'll keep focusing on stopping the white power terrorist THE [sic] ARE ACTUALLY ATTACKING US!"

His declaration sparked backlash. But his father and fellow Antifa supporter, Attorney General Keith Ellison, explained that his son's "official" support was just a "comment" about the DOJ and President Trump designating Antifa as a terrorist organization.[202]

---

200. Minneapolis City Council. (2017, December 29). About Jeremiah Ellison. City of Minneapolis. http://www2.minneapolismn.gov/ward5/about-jeremiah

201. Ellison, J. [@jeremiah4north]. (2020, May 31). *I hereby declare, officially, my support for ANTIFA.* [Tweet] Twitter. https://twitter.com/jeremiah4north/status/1267152043313172482

202. Office of Public Affairs. (2020, May 31). Attorney General William P. Barr's statement on riots and domestic terrorism. *Department of Justice.*

A few days later, Jeremiah told his constituents and the residents of Minneapolis about the city council's plans for policing:[203]

> "We are going to dismantle the Minneapolis Police Department. And when we're done, we're not simply gonna glue it back together. We are going to dramatically rethink how we approach public safety and emergency response. It's really past due."

Jeremiah encourages people who live and work in Minneapolis to reach out to him. He even keeps open office hours for "Coffee with Jeremiah":

> "We'll have the chance to dream, collaborate, and create solutions together. No issue is too big or small over coffee."

But he was never available to talk to me about the staggering crime in the area he represents. However, the stats say everything there is to say about Jeremiah's "rethinking" of public safety.

---

203. Ellison, J. [@jeremiah4north]. (2020, June 4). *We are going to dismantle the Minneapolis Police Department [...]* [Tweet] Twitter. https://twitter.com/jeremiah4north/status/1268598536234508288

## Murders in Ward 5, Represented by Jeremiah Ellison

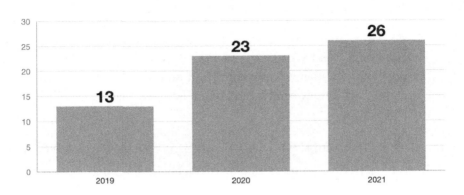

*The number of "murder and non-negligent manslaughter" cases in Ward 5 during the tenure of Minneapolis City Council Member Jeremiah Ellison from 2019 through 2021, the years before and after the death of George Floyd (Source: Minneapolis Crime Dashboard).*

## Shots Fired Calls in Ward 5, Represented by Jeremiah Ellison

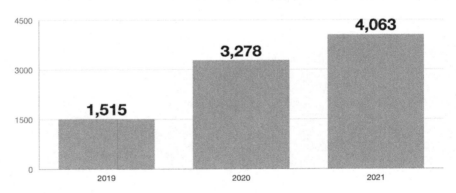

*Shots fired calls in Ward 5 from 2019 through 2021 in Ward 5 during the "leadership" of Minneapolis City Council Member Jeremiah Ellison, an "official" supporter of Antifa (Source: Minneapolis Crime Dashboard).*

## Mayor Jacob Frey

As a former civil rights attorney, it's not surprising that Minneapolis Mayor Jacob Frey jumped to conclusions after the death of George Floyd. However, instead of inspiring calm, he inspired outrage. Even though he has yet to acknowledge them, many of his failures have led to catastrophic consequences.[204] Frey let one incident define the history of Minneapolis for years to come. And while he may not have taken direct action to defund the police department, he did nothing to stop it from falling apart. Frey's political moves have left the people who live and work in Minnesota's largest city fearing for their safety every day. Giving up the Third Precinct and leaving officers to fend for themselves prompted an exodus among the ranks that shows no signs of slowing down. Officers like Sam Belcourt and Scott Creighton, supervisors like Kim Voss and Gary Nelson, and so many others were left abandoned during the riots. They soon left the department along with hundreds of other officers. Consequently, the constant crime and the 911 call wait times became so unbearable that several citizens sued the city to force the hiring of more officers. This isn't what the right side of history should look like.[205]

Looking back, when Frey was campaigning to become mayor in 2017, he wanted support from the police union (behind the scenes, of course). Bob will be the first to tell you that when it comes to union politics, whether someone was a democrat or a republican, officers supported whoever supported them. In return, Frey promised to hire 100 more police officers. However, in what seems like just one of his many lies, Frey apparently didn't support them—and didn't keep his word.

---

204. Review of lawlessness and government responses to Minnesota's 2020 Riots. (2020, October 8). *Joint Transportation and Judiciary and Public Safety Committee Minnesota Senate.*

205. Navaratil, L. (2022, October 3). Minneapolis, 8 North Side residents agree to end police staffing lawsuit. *Star Tribune.*

## Number of Minneapolis Police Officers—40% Decrease

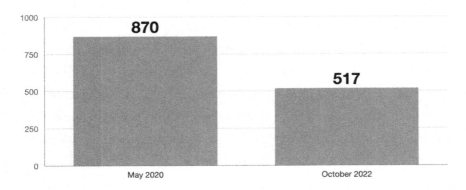

*The number of MPD officers decreased 40% from May 2020 (before the riots) and October 2022 (Source: Police Officers Federation of Minneapolis).*

## Murders During Mayor Frey's "Leadership"

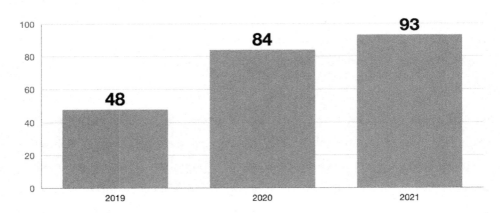

*The number of "murder and non-negligent manslaughter" cases during the last three complete years under Mayor Frey's leadership 2019-2021 (Source: Minneapolis Crime Dashboard).*

## Attorney General Keith Ellison

In winning a conviction in the trial of Derek Chauvin, Ellison made it seem like he was making history:[206]

> "We presented a remarkable, historic case. We had the sole burden of proof, and history shows that winning cases like these is hard."

*The New York Times* touted his triumph as though he achieved the impossible:

> "In prosecuting the Chauvin case, Mr. Ellison assembled a team of outside lawyers to handle motions and the presentation of evidence and testimony, and the outcome was a rarity in America: Very few prosecutors have ever convicted a police officer of murder for killing on the job."

However, in 2019, former Minneapolis Police Officer Mohamed Noor was convicted of murder. So, Ellison's "historic case" might not have been so historic. In just two years, Ellison has taken over the prosecution of five former police officers: the four officers related to the death of George Floyd; and former Brooklyn Center Police Officer Kim Potter in the accidental shooting of Duante Wright.[207] If this sounds like Ellison had a vendetta against the police, judging by his own words, it certainly seems that way.

Ellison has long held anti-cop and anti-government beliefs. In 1989, during a protest outside the mayor's office in downtown Minneapolis, Ellison called out MPD officers saying:

---

206. Arango, T. (2021, April 21). 'Gentle steering of the ship': How Keith Ellison led the prosecution of Chauvin. *The New York Times*.

207. Blume, P. (2021, May 21). Attorney General takes over prosecution of Kim Potter for Duante Wright shooting death. Fox 9. *KMSP*.

"These people [MPD officers] are vicious, we're talking about wolves in sheep's clothing."[208]

In many ways, Ellison's conviction against Derek Chauvin also seems like retribution for what happened to Rodney King in 1991. In discussing Chauvin's conviction, Ellison explained:[209]

"I was never convinced we were going to win this case until we heard the verdict of guilty. I remember what happened in the Rodney King case when I was a pretty young man, young lawyer.

And I remember how devastated I felt when I heard that the jury acquitted those officers. Whenever an officer is charged with an offense, particularly when the victim is a person of color, it's just rare that there's any accountability. And so, there was every moment of this case, I thought, 'What are we missing? What haven't we done?'"

In 1992, after the acquittal of the four LAPD officers involved in the Rodney King incident, Ellison seems to have become obsessed. This all happened in Los Angeles. But you'd never know it from the protests Ellison led on behalf of the Coalition for Police Accountability in Minneapolis. Ellison said the acquittals were "criminal" and a "cover up" and it was "evil!"

Ellison has also attacked "the culture" of the police union and MPD officers while ignoring the rampant gang violence going on throughout "Murderapolis" at the time.[210] In speaking out against tough-on-crime legislation in the early '90s, Ellison proclaimed:[211]

---

208. Kerr, E. (1989, February 17). Protest on police brutality outside mayor Don Fraser's office. *MPR*.
209. Pelley, S. (2021, April 26). 60 Minutes interviews the prosecutors of Derek Chauvin. *CBS News*.
210. Fudge, T. (1992, December 23). Minneapolis police federation culture. *MPR*.
211. Kerr, E. (1993, December 14). Cops and the courts: Justice(?) for victims and criminals. *MPR*.

"I believe that race and crime are fundamental stabilizing political forces for certain people and certain people profit from it."

Ironically, 30 years later, with five convictions against police officers, it seems Ellison's career has profited from "historic" wins against certain people—police officers. If Chauvin's case was about revenge, retribution, and settling the score, then Ellison seems to be on the right side of history in his own mind. With the rampant crime—and soaring opioid overdoses—in Minnesota, some people are starting to see through the lies. In fact, it seems Ellison could use a "dose of reality" himself.

### Opioid-related Deaths During Ellison's "Dose of Reality" Campaign

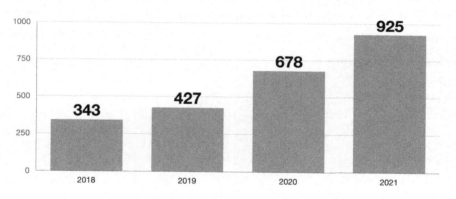

*The number of opioid-related deaths that have occurred while Keith Ellison has served as attorney general and promoted the "Dose of Reality" anti-opioid campaign (Source: Minnesota Department of Health).*

## Governor Tim Walz

During the riots, no other so-called leader failed the state of Minnesota more than Governor Tim Walz. In many ways, he lit the match for chaos and crime across the country. There is a mountain of evidence to support making such bold claims.[212] More than a few reports underscore Walz' failures, including how he mishandled calling in the National Guard and played political blame games while people were suffering the worst riots ever in Minnesota—and the most expensive riots in American history. Walz' prejudice also caused irreparable damage. He was making historical connections without knowing all the facts and seemed to be doing everything he could to promote the narrative the media and the Left were perpetrating. Just two weeks after the incident, Walz issued the following proclamation.[213] It could've been a sincere gesture. But he seemed to be exploiting the death of George Floyd for the sake of division and identity politics.

---

212. The following 86-page report reviewed more than 2,400 documents; City of Minneapolis: An after-action review of city agencies' responses to activities directly following George Floyd's death on May 25, 2020. (2022, March 7). *Hillard Heintze*. See also, Review of lawlessness and government responses to Minnesota's 2020 Riots. (2020, October 8). *Joint Transportation and Judiciary and Public Safety Committee Minnesota Senate.*
213. Governor Tim Walz orders moment of silence for George Floyd. (2020, June 9). *Office of Governor Tim Walz and Lt. Governor Peggy Flanagan.* https://mn.gov/governor/news/?id=1055-435187

# STATE *of* MINNESOTA

## *Proclamation*

WHEREAS:     George Floyd was a beloved father, son, brother, uncle, cousin, nephew, neighbor, and friend; and

WHEREAS:     The world watched in horror as George Floyd's humanity was taken away from him; and

WHEREAS:     The local, national, and international mourning for George Floyd is about more than one tragic incident; and

WHEREAS:     George Floyd's death is the symptom of a disease – the result of generations of systemic racism that threaten the dignity of our state's Black communities, Indigenous communities, and communities of color; and

WHEREAS:     Minnesota has a dark history of inflicting violence on Black communities, Indigenous communities, and communities of color, notably with the mass hanging of 38 Dakota men in Mankato on December 26, 1862, the largest mass execution in United States history, and the lynching of three black men, Elias Clayton, Elmer Jackson, and Isaac McGhie, in Duluth on June 15, 1920; and

WHEREAS:     We will not wake up one day and have the disease of systemic racism cured; we must do everything in our power to come together to deconstruct generations of systemic racism in our state so that every Minnesotan – Black, Indigenous, Brown, or White – can be safe and thrive.

NOW, THEREFORE, I, TIM WALZ, Governor of Minnesota, do hereby order a moment of silence in the State of Minnesota, at 11:00 AM on Tuesday, June 9, 2020 for 8 minutes and 46 seconds, to honor the life of George Floyd and the lives of every person cut short due to systems of racism and discrimination in Minnesota.

IN WITNESS WHEREOF, I have hereunto set my hand and caused the Great Seal of the State of Minnesota to be affixed at the State Capitol this 8th day of June.

_____

GOVERNOR

*Proclamation issued by Minnesota Governor Tim Walz on June 9, 2020 requesting Minnesotans to spend 8 minutes and 46 seconds in silence to honor George Floyd.*

## President Joe Biden

When George Floyd was arrested and died, then-presidential candidate Joe Biden instantly tried to become an outspoken leader for social justice. He began urging police reforms and demanding Congress act with "no more delays" and "no more excuses." He also promised the American public:[214]

> "I won't fan the flames of hate... I will seek to heal the racial wounds that have long plagued this country—not use them for political gain."

The next day, Biden gave a speech that symbolically began with "I can't breathe"—the last words George Floyd reportedly said before he died.[215] He seemed to be doing exactly what he promised *not* to do. Biden also made another promise: he would establish a police oversight committee within his first 100 days if he were elected president.[216] Since then, Biden may have become president, but he failed to keep his word. He did not establish the committee in his first 100 days or the first two years for that matter. In May of 2022, he reversed course when he stood among a group of police chiefs from across the country and begged them to spend government funds to help reduce crime rates. In completely contradicting himself, Biden was now offering *more funding* for police officers and *without* the additional oversight he promised. Figuring out whether Biden has ended up on the right side of history isn't difficult. However, figuring out precisely just how bad crime has become under the Biden administration isn't an easy task. That's because the FBI still hasn't collected 2021 crime data from nearly 40% of the police departments in America. But even with so much missing data, there are still

214. Wootson, C. R. (2022, May 23). Two years after Floyd's death, little movement on police reform in Washington. *The Washington Post.*

215. Joe Biden's remarks on civil unrest and nationwide protests. (2020, June 2). *CNN.*

216. Erickson, B., & Quinn, M. (2020, June 1). Biden vows to set up police oversight board if elected. *CBS News.*

shocking indications that crime has become much worse under Biden's "leadership." He's obviously overlooking the violence that has tragically affected cops and citizens alike.

### Law Enforcement Officers Killed in 2020 and 2021: 58% Increase

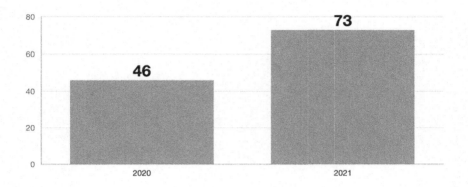

*In 2020, 46 law enforcement officers were feloniously killed in the line of duty. That number tragically increased 58% to 73 in 2021 according to FBI UCR and NIBRS crime data.*

### Estimated Murders in 2019 and 2021: 39% Increase*

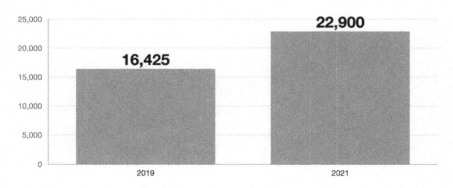

*Murders in America increased by an estimated 39% from 16,425 in 2019 (the year before George Floyd was arrested and died) and 2021 (the year after) according to FBI UCR and NIBRS crime data. Data from law enforcement agencies covering nearly 40% of the population, including NYPD and LAPD, have yet to be reported.*

## State Representative John Thompson

John Thompson is no longer a member of the democratic party of Minnesota.[217]

---

217. His controversies are too numerous to list.